Spirit-Led Evangelism

ISBN 978-1-908154-05-7

Published in the USA by:
Oracle Publishing Services
Maricopa, Arizona
www.oracle-ministries.org

Spirit-Led Evangelism

POWERFUL STORIES & INSIGHTS
FOR EVERYONE WISHING TO BRING
GOD'S LOVE & LIGHT
TO A HURTING WORLD

By
Ella Onakoya

ENDORSEMENTS

I first met Ella Onakoya in Thailand during an Operation Extreme Love School that my ministry was hosting. Participants were gathered from all around the world. Why was Ella there? Because she longed to bring Christ's glorious love and light into the darkness of human trafficking and the sex tourism industry that enveloped the streets we labored in -- and she did! Since that time Ella and I have become friends. She is like a spiritual daughter to me and a true evangelist with a heart that burns for the lost, revival, and a demonstration of the Spirit of God. You will be refreshed, empowered, and equipped as you read her book that is full of faith-filled Spirit-directed writing. Congratulations Ella - well done!

~ Patricia King
Founder, XPministries

In her book, ***Spirit-Led Evangelism***, Ella combines both biblical truth and lessons learnt through practical experience of sharing the good news of Jesus Christ to present a compelling and heartfelt call to the church. Through her personal testimonies, she shares how her calling and passion for sharing the message of Jesus Christ came not through a sense of obligation, but rather, through a personal and life changing encounter with the

love of God that was too good to keep to herself. Her insights and encouragements will inspire you to have the passion for sharing your faith stirred and sharpened.

~ Tom Allsop
Associate Pastor, Catch the Fire London

This truly is a book on how to be led by the Holy Spirit and how to minister the love of the Lord to people.

Ella Onakoya has shown us, through examples from her own life, how the Lord has taught her in following and flowing with the River of God.

She has shared with us how to connect with people, how to pray and listen to the Lord. Her teaching empowers us to pray and minister to people more effectively wherever we are.

This is the call for today, to encounter the heart of God every day. To go out and let the Lord lead us to someone He is wanting to touch with His love. This is for each one of us, so let's go out and evangelise by the Spirit! Our lives will never be the same and together we can impact the world!

~ Dr. Mark R. Van Gundy
Senior Pastor, Church of Destiny
London, England

Spirit-Led Evangelism is a cutting-edge book that will inspire you, challenge you and provoke you to reach the lost in our nations. Ella Onakoya shares her inspiring journey, as a revivalist and evangelist in many nations. After her sister shared the life-changing gospel with Ella and she experienced a supernatural encounter in her room as she prayed she never turned back.

Even when she had no platform to minister, she made the streets her pulpit, reaching out to her neighbors, the homeless, giving encouraging words to those who needed it most. Throughout the book Ella shares how fear never held her back from sharing the gospel in hard ground places in Muslim communities in London, and in villages in Africa and other parts of the world.

Not only is ***Spirit-Led Evangelism*** a read you will not want to put down, it also is a true inspiration of the Holy Spirit. With her practical everyday examples you will be challenged whether you are a new believer, or a seasoned evangelist. Ella demonstrates her compassion for lost souls and the broken. I was touched as I read the story of Brian a homeless man who had no friends or family to speak of, yet Ella became the only one who reached out to him, led him to the Lord and was the only one at his funeral when he died.

I highly recommend ***Spirit-Led Evangelism*** and author Ella Onakoya to my family, friends and fellow ministers of the gospel. You will be challenged by Ella's walk, boldness and faith in her saviour. Along with practical everyday examples you will receive a mighty impartation from this book and will go forth with the gospel!

~ Kira Mulindwa
Founder and Director, Unquenchable Ministries

DEDICATION

I would like to dedicate this book to God who inspired me to write this book.

To Jesus Christ whose death on the cross and His love for mankind motivated me to write a book on what is closest to His heart.

To my mother, a true inspiration who has passed on to heaven, and to my loving family - My Dad and my siblings, Modupe, Oluseun, Busola, Funmilayo, Oluseyi, Toyin.

ACKNOWLEDGEMENTS

I would like to thank God who gave me the strength and fortitude to write this book. A special thank you to all the pastors who opened up the doors to invite me to minister in all the countries where a move of God took place, which saved and set many free. I am thankful to God for their openness in giving me the freedom to allow the Holy Spirit to move in all the ways He chose to. I would like to thank Pastor Adeniyi Ajibola who has been such an inspiring and spiritual father to me throughout the years.

A very special thank you to a most amazing mother anyone could ever have – Debola. The powerful legacy of love, faith, prayer, and humility she left behind (as she has now gone to be with the Lord) has been one of the most powerful inspirations for this book.

A thank you to the rest of my family, whose love, support and friendship has strengthened and refreshed me through all the years.

A very big thank you to all those who read the manuscript and helped with advice, endorsements, prayer, and editing.

A special thank you to Patricia King, a true spiritual mother, who has mentored and prayed for me throughout the years, and who wrote a true mother's endorsement for this book.

A special thank you to Kira Mulindwa, a dear friend who also took the time to read and endorse the book. I also want to thank Pastor Tom Allsop who has also given time into the reading and endorsing it, as well as Mark Van Gundy, one of the Senior Pastors in the London churches. Thanks also to James Maloney, who has also demonstrated such a father heart in giving helpful advice and encouragement while writing ***Spirit-Led Evangelism.***

A very special thank you to David Powell, who has helped in so many ways with this book. I am thankful for the hours he poured into advising me and helping to edit it, simply to be a blessing to my ministry. I am grateful beyond words.

I am also thankful to Mark Jeffrey whose invaluable advice has also helped me to write ***Spirit-Led Evangelism.*** I'm thankful to other friends, including Tayo, Yvonne, Rachel, Brian, Fabian, and others who have encouraged me greatly while writing it.

TABLE OF CONTENTS

PREFACE

Without any doubt, I believe God's heart is that all would be saved and that all would come to the knowledge of the truth through believing in Jesus for the forgiveness of their sins and through personal relationship with Him as their Saviour.

When travelling and ministering in different nations to folks who need Jesus with many diverse needs and challenges, I watched with amazement and delight how the Lord brought conviction to hearts, even those hardened by sin and shame, to the point of believing in him wholeheartedly for their salvation. Some of these events took place in nations that had not had a lot of breakthroughs in the area of harvest of souls. A number of people of other faiths were saved during these events.

With all these supernatural events and breakthroughs taking place in different nations and also while training churches on Spirit-led Evangelism to help equip them to see breakthroughs in day to day evangelism, I started getting requests to write a book regarding this topic. Finally in July 2012, I started to write this book, using my experiences and testimonies to help and encourage others to walk in breakthrough in the area of evangelism.

It is my hope and intention that those who read this book, while reading it, takes a journey into an adventure with God knowing that beyond their wildest dreams all things are possible for those who believe.

This book is for an army of everyday believers that God is raising up, it is for leaders and pastors who are hungry to hear the heartbeat of God and follow His desire to reach the lost wherever they might be. It is for those who are hungry for revival and have been praying and crying out for the Lord of the harvest to send, equip and release labourers into the work of the harvest.

This book is for those whose heart and voice echo Isaiah when the Lord asked him, 'Whom shall I send?' and he answered 'Here I am. Send me!' (Isaiah 6: 8).

These are the ones who understand that loving Jesus is about laying down their lives daily in order to love those He loves the most. To love many to life and to follow the Lamb of God whatever the cost is the call of this hour.

As you read this book, it is my prayer that you will enter into a deeper level of your walk with Jesus in intimacy, love, and sacrifice, as well as obedience to Jesus' call upon your lives to become end-time harvesters. I also pray this book helps many walk in greater breakthroughs of bringing the lost to Jesus through the accounts of God's miracles, testimonies, and keys to become effective witnesses for Jesus that are laid out in this book.

Chapter One

My Background – From Darkness to Light

CHAPTER ONE

Born in England to a Nigerian father and mother, I must confess I remember nothing of my time there as I was just under a year old when my parents took me and my two siblings back to live in Nigeria. We settled in Lagos and I remember growing up in an atmosphere where laughter and jokes were so much a part of our loving family. I also remember my Mum as being a very God-fearing woman who appeared to know the Lord. Even though ours was a home where we went to church religiously, I knew very little of Jesus and had not experienced personal salvation.

I liked the idea of outwardly proclaiming to be a Christian and being known as a "good girl" even though I did not know Jesus personally. I remember that as a young child, one of my favourite occasions while being at church was the prophetic time when a minister was given the opportunity to prophesy, usually for about an hour. Alas, I enjoyed this time not because I enjoyed the prophetic words but because the prophetic time at church allowed me to rest my head on the table while I pretended to piously listen to the prophetic words. But I would soon fall fast asleep, only to wake up just as the prophecy ended. Then I would give the loudest "Amen" as if I had been listening all along. That was me having a façade of holiness but with a gaping emptiness inside.

My childhood was also marked by traumatic times which began at school. I started going to school at the age of five at a local primary school near my home. I remember putting on my school uniform with butterflies in my stomach anxiously awaiting my first day. As a young child I was extremely small for my age; I soon became the target of intense bullying at school by those who saw me as an easy object upon whom to vent their pent-up rage.

These bullying sessions would range from being slapped constantly to being ambushed on my way home where I was beaten repeatedly till I fell to the ground. One day I was standing at an assembly line with other kids when one of the boys pretended he was a bull. Running towards me in full force, he smashed his head into my stomach. (In his mind, his head was a bull's horn.) I doubled up in agonising pain but by then this had become a commonplace occurrence to me and I could not even dream of telling a teacher or my parents as I felt this would only make the kids antagonize me more.

I moved on to an all girls secondary school and the bullying was pretty much the same. Again I was marked out for bullying for different reasons. I was still very small for my age; I was told I had physical features which irritated other kids – namely what was described as a large forehead and big teeth. I was also top of the class which brought extreme jealousy. Again I was slapped, beaten up constantly, and also mentally abused.

My classmates soon devised ways of benefiting from my intelligence. The teachers we had at school would threaten to beat the students that didn't get answers right. As a result students who sat close to me would whisper to me to give them answers to questions if I didn't want to be beaten up after school.

All of these situations caused me to become extremely depressed. I remember being alone at home and feeling anguish well up in me. I started to self- harm by hitting my forehead on the hard concrete wall of our Nigerian home. I wanted the pain I was inflicting on myself to deaden the pain inside of me but of course it did not work because only Jesus can fill up the vacuums in our souls and only He can permanently take away our pain. Things got worse when I became suicidal. Acting on the voices I heard constantly in my head that I was no good, I decided to act on it by writing a note where I detailed my plans to end my life and commit suicide by overdosing on pills. Thankfully my Mum found the note and talked me out of it.

Indeed, I am sharing this story of my background not to invite feelings of pity but to encourage those reading this book to give glory to a God who can deliver us from the deepest darkness and pain once we come to Him. I also believe that oftentimes the enemy is somehow able to sense God's impending greatness in our lives; threatened, he tries to snuff it out before it manifests, using strategies to intimidate and discourage us. But of course, Satan is no match for the unending love of the Father who never stops until we are brought home to His heart through Jesus Christ.

My opportunity to meet my Saviour came through my older sister who, on one of her visits home from the university, told us she was now born again. This meant very little to me as I knew very little about personal salvation, but I was curious enough to seek a meeting with her to ask her what she meant by being born again. I also wanted to know how her experience made her so different from the rest of us.

She explained that God wanted a relationship with us rather than works. He wants us to receive salvation by grace through Jesus

rather than trying to earn salvation through our own works. She told me that everyone had sinned and fallen short of the glory of God, but that Jesus came to take away our sins through His death on the cross and restore us back to the Father's glory. For the first time I saw how we regain the glory of God through salvation and faith through the finished work of the cross. I scarcely knew how to contain myself at this news but still I could not believe it could be so easy to obtain salvation.

I was amazed to hear that God wanted a relationship with me. I asked my sister what I needed to do to obtain salvation. She explained that I needed to say a prayer to God asking Him to forgive my sins, and that I needed to have a personal relationship with Jesus by receiving him as Lord and Saviour in my heart.

This is where I would advise those who express doubts as to whether the salvation prayer really works to understand that when we ask Jesus into our hearts, He has the power to change us by removing the old nature from within us and giving us the righteousness of God.

> *"Behold I stand at the door and knock; if anyone hears My voice and open the door, I will come in to him and will dine with him, and he with Me".* Revelation 3:20 NASB

All the Lord needs is an invitation. So when someone comes to the Lord during street evangelism, for example, trust that the sinners' prayer, said from the heart, is answered by the Saviour who is able to save those who come to Him. Do all you can to connect them to a local church, by all means, and also pray for them that Christ may be fully formed in them as they mature in Him, but believe that Jesus is able to truly save them through their prayer of repentance and faith in Him as Saviour.

I have heard believers express doubt and wonder if a person who has said a sinner's prayer is truly saved and sometimes some are reluctant to lead people to the Lord for this reason. Do not doubt that the Lord is able to do a work of salvation in those who ask him. We do our part in presenting the full gospel of the cross and trusting the Lord to save those who reach out to Him.

After my sister advised me to say the sinner's prayer, I went into my room and knelt down by my bed. I prayed and asked God to forgive my sins and invited Jesus to come into my heart to be my Lord and Saviour. I scarcely knew what to expect but I opened my eyes after saying the prayers and I remember wondering where I was because the room I was in suddenly became very bright, almost as if it was birthed with the presence of God's light from heaven.

I did not know what that was then but that was His glory. I felt the heavy weight of darkness that often seemed to sit on my head and darken my thoughts leave me. In its place I felt God's peace flood my heart. I felt the Spirit of joy flood my heart. I was inexpressibly happy. I felt the love of my Saviour for me and I fell in love with Him. I had just met my Saviour but I was madly in love with him and I instantly felt released from all depression and all suicidal thoughts. God also gave me the ability to forgive all those who had hurt me.

I believe the Lord allowed me to feel such an instant transformation because He wanted me to understand the reality of the new birth, and in that experience, to know what I had been given from above so that with boldness I would be able to share the truth of His gospel through His love and power in me.

> *"If anyone is in Christ, he is a new creature, the old things passed away; behold, new things have come".*
>
> 2 Corinthians 5:17 NASB

> *"But you are a chosen people, a royal priesthood, a holy nation, God's Special possession, that you may declare the praises of him who called you out of darkness into his wonderful light".*
> 1 Peter 2:9

This was not just my salvation experience but this was also the beginning of my call to reach the lost. At fifteen years of age after experiencing salvation when I invited Jesus to come into my heart, I also felt commissioned by Jesus to release His salvation to all those who need Him. Within a few weeks and months, I had started to minister and share the gospel with as many as I could find on the streets of Lagos and in houses, knocking from door to door where I was welcomed by many. Filled with the fire and love of Jesus, as I spoke many became believers, often with tears streaming down their faces. They would become full of joy when they understood the reality of their salvation. They were also filled with the Holy Spirit.

It was my practice to wake up and leave home early in the morning and not come back home till nightfall because of the many souls the Lord was calling me to attend to. Some seemed to sense, that coupled with the fire and love of God, I was also carrying the presence of the fear of the Lord. One of those was a woman who lived around our neighbourhood who started to weep and started to confess her sins loudly, asking God to forgive her as I approached her. With no condemning words spoken from me, it could only have been the convicting fire of the Holy Ghost Himself that elicited such a response. I gently told her how to get right with God through Jesus and that the Lord was able to forgive all sins. Soon she gave her heart to Him.

The early part of my Christianity as a teenager was evidenced with a high sensitivity to the Holy Spirit where I would often hear the Father's heart so clearly and it was always drawing me

to love, care for, and bring to His son those He loves so much. If we will only listen to His heartbeat more closely, surely we will hear His heart call crying out for those He loves and sent His Son to die for.

I remember how I also prayed for the physically sick. I could never forget the wells of compassion that rose in me one day as I sat outside of a school library and saw the most physically deformed man I ever knew walk into the compound. From head to toe, he was covered in lumps that oozed liquid. One of his eyes was missing and was shut tight, oozing pus continuously. Many shuddered and I wept out loud uncontrollably. After he left, I asked for his address and someone took me to where he stayed at a carpenter's shed. He had been evicted cruelly from his home as many tenants claimed to have been too frightened by his appearance to stay with him. He introduced himself to me as Tunde.

After I led him to the Lord, I started to call him Brother Tunde. I visited with him for about a year and though I did not see him physically healed, it was so important for me to show him the love and compassion that had been so missing in his life. When visiting with him, I would often share a meal with him; we would talk and share the scriptures together. I believe the very heartbeat of Jesus is love and we need a daily immersion of His love in our hearts to effectively love the unsaved into His kingdom and disciple those He brings into our lives.

In this chapter, I have shared much about my background, especially how I came to know Jesus. I have shared my story to show that often those the Lord calls are not the most knowledgeable or the wisest according to the worldly standards, but rather He reaches out and uses people like myself – those who previously were steeped in shame, despair, and darkness,

then transformed through the life of His Son, Jesus. If you were ever in this category, you are a candidate to be used by God in this hour of great harvest. Not that the Lord cannot use even the wise of this world as He is not a discriminator of persons, but like Saul in the Bible who became Paul, even the wise of this world must count everything as loss for the surpassing worth of knowing Christ Jesus. for no flesh must glory in His presence.

Chapter Two

The Legacy of Prayer Brings Revival

In writing this book, I believe it is fitting to include God's divinely orchestrated events that took place when growing up in Lagos, Nigeria shortly before my move to England in 1999. In the first chapter, I shared that I was born in London, to Nigerian parents who took me and my siblings back to Nigeria when I was still quite young. God used my time growing up in Lagos in a lot of ways, to train and prepare me for the work of revival, especially for the years ahead as I moved back to England in 1999 to continue my studies abroad.

As you read this book, prayer is often mentioned as a key to the moves of God in different nations as I travelled to minister there. I certainly learnt the value of prayer from very early on. The role of prayer in any move or revival cannot be emphasized enough.

From childhood, I had had the benefits of having a praying mother who prayed often and fervently and with great faith. Her life of prayer was such a great testament and example to many, that during the celebration of her life at her funeral two years ago in Nigeria, one of those who came up to comment on my Mum had this to say about her...

"I often heard the prayers of Mama in the early hours of the morning, every morning, and hearing her prayers made me get up and pray too. But one morning, I listened for these prayers

and heard nothing, I later discovered that Mama had passed away"

Although my Mum's passing away was a sad event for us, we were happy to have been blessed with such a rich legacy of prayer. We remembered how she prayed constantly when we were kids. Hers were not prayers that were just mouthed mechanically but they were prayers that were full of profound faith.

There were several examples of her faith-filled prayers. Once, when we were growing up, she had befriended a particular Muslim family (she often practiced friendship evangelism). She noticed the family often did not have enough food to eat and one of their kids had sadly died of malnutrition. We were not rich ourselves but she offered to take care of one of their girls within our own family to take the strain off their financial burdens. The girl came into our home showing symptoms of tuberculosis, coughing and spitting blood frequently. My Dad was worried that we might be infected but my Mum declared our house a non-infection zone as she believed we were living in the realms of Psalm 91 in God's secret place.

We all continued to live together in close proximity. I watched my Mum pray for the girl and share the gospel with her. She stopped coughing, became completely healed, healthy and became a Christian too along with members of her family.

Another time there was an outbreak of meningitis in Nigeria and many were told to be vaccinated against this deadly disease. Many did indeed die of this terrible disease at the time but my Mum, with her radical faith, calmly told us that we did not need vaccination as God's word in Psalm 91 had promised us that no plagues will come near our tent, and truly we did not get vaccinated and never became ill.

It was watching her lifestyle of faith that made me stay and take care of a bed-ridden lady racked with tuberculosis in a flat I shared with others shortly in London even when some fled in fear of possible infection. I was not afraid of being infected as I had watched my Mum first-hand as she took care of an infected girl in close proximity who later became healed.

I tried to live the reality of living in God's presence which protects against all diseases the way my Mum did. I knew God's word was real and I tried to cultivate living in His presence by living in the realm of prayers fuelled by the word and promises of God, one of which is Psalm 91.

Nigeria at the time had an epidemic of armed robbers who would gain entry into homes and not only steal but kill at will. As soon as we moved into the neighbourhood, we received letters from armed robbers telling us to get ready for a visit from them. We knew what that meant and the armed robbers had wanted us to be intimidated. My Mum simply called us to make prayer decrees daily to decree our home impenetrable to the enemy and we never had a visit from the armed robbers!

I believe these examples of prayer and faith as exemplified by my mother can greatly benefit us who are working in the harvest field today. Sometimes we might be called by the Lord to work in the mission field where disease and dangers are rife. While it is good and wise to take all necessary precautions to be protected, we ought to know the reality of what God's abiding presence can do to protect us at such times. When we nurture His presence through prayer in our lives, we begin to live more and more in the atmosphere of heaven, where heaven invades our lives. Angels are dispatched to protect us from evil and God's presence within us keeps sicknesses and diseases at bay. This is important

because we do need to be strong and healthy when working in God's harvest field, and the Lord has made provision for this.

Recently, I returned from a ministry trip from Nigeria to London where I currently reside and I travelled to minister in New York almost immediately afterwards. I had misplaced some of my anti-malaria tablets which I was to continue taking even after my trip to Nigeria. I was in New York and had no access to get this medication, which is only available by prescription. I started to develop symptoms of extreme weakness and my body began to get increasingly hot. I had been bitten a lot by mosquitoes while away and usually the immune system is significantly weaker when one has not lived in a malaria prone-zone for a number of years. I invited the Lord's presence and decreed healing into my body and I became well.

When the Lord leads us to minister and travel in disease-prone areas, we can live a lifestyle of prayer, cultivating His presence which will release protection and healing to us. At other times, I had been led to minister to those of another faith or others who had been very hostile to me, but the presence of the Lord has intervened and caused a mellowing of hearts and calmness in the hearts of those who had initially opposed me.

I remember my personal prayer times after I got saved. Praying for me was not about establishing regimented times in which I committed certain time for prayer. I was so abandoned to the move of the Holy Spirit within me that I would feel the unction within me to pray and was often awakened in the midnight hours to pray. As I got up from my bed and began to pray, it would often seem as if rivers of prayers and intercessions poured out of me. Lost in prayer and in the presence of God, it seemed as if I was covered in the realms of eternity where there was no measurement of time. Oftentimes, it was my Dad's voice calling

me to make breakfast before I went to school that would alert me to the fact I had been praying for six hours! Those prayer times just seemed like moments as I was lost in the presence of the Lord.

I believe those prayer times significantly paved the way for the work of God in the nations as he is leading and directing me now. What an invaluable legacy of prayer my mother taught and imparted into us and what a wise investment it was indeed to invest all those times and hours of prayer starting from the early years I was saved. I strongly believe the Lord is calling us to re-dig wells of prayer and intercession again and cultivate a lifestyle of prayer to see revival come. 1 Thessalonians 5:17 admonishes us to pray constantly. Ephesians 6:18 also calls us to pray on all occasions with all manners of prayers and requests.

Legacies of prayer impacting a move of God in Lagos, Nigeria 1996-1999

God used my mother and the powerful unction of the Holy Spirit to show me the powerful impact of prayer since from childhood and as I grew up after I was saved. God also orchestrated events that took place in the Redeemed Christian Church of God, which was the church I attended in Nigeria. not only to bring a mighty move in a part of Lagos but also to impart to me much wisdom regarding the strategies of prayers that can impact those seeking breakthroughs in their cities or areas of ministry.

I look back at my time as part of the Redeemed Christian Church of God as a very important part of my life, especially with regard to the event that took place leading me and others to become part of a church plant. The events that followed were orchestrated by God as a training camp in many ways. The legacy of prayer and spiritual warfare was very important and valuable for the work ahead.

I learnt that by travail and prayer, the will of the Father could be born within a very short time and even in a day according to Isaiah 66: *"Can a country be born in a day?... no sooner is Zion in labor than she gives birth to her children."* God also taught me warfare against persistent and demonic opposition.

I and others witnessed the move of God which released dominion in an area of Lagos, Nigeria. I was part of a large church that was headed by a pastor who was very charismatic and full of wisdom. There were various departments in the church that offered training and discipleship and it also had one of the strongest prayer teams I had met anywhere.

Oftentimes as I walked around the outskirts of the church on the streets, I began to feel a burden in my heart that so many outside of the church needed to be reached with the love and power of Jesus with the kingdom of God demonstrated in love and power to them. I felt in my heart that while the church had excelled in training, discipleship and intercession, the next step was to impact those around us with the kingdom of God.

I began to feel such a burden from the Lord to begin to spend time interceding for the heart to reach the lost to be imparted to the local church, and for an urgency for the need for a harvest of souls outside the four walls of the church to be felt. The bride within the local church was becoming mature but I felt the call to go out and release the light within us to those who needed Christ the most. God has a plan that when we are obedient to the nudging of His Spirit to pray His heart for the situation He has placed within us, then His plans and purposes can be birthed.

Isaiah 66: 7- 9 has proved to be true time and time again:

'Before she goes into labor,
she gives birth;

before the pains come upon her,
she delivers a son.
8 Who has ever heard of such things?
Who has ever seen things like this?
Can a country be born in a day
or a nation be brought forth in a moment?
Yet no sooner is Zion in labor
than she gives birth to her children.
9 Do I bring to the moment of birth
and not give delivery?" says the Lord.
"Do I close up the womb
when I bring to delivery?" says your God.

I started to pray and intercede with a strong intensity fuelled by the Spirit of God for my local church to come into the fullness of God's heart's desire for the communities and souls around the church. The burden of this prayer was such that I could not shut out the Spirit's unction each time I was led to pray. Sometimes, it was when I was about to watch a favourite TV programme that the urge or unction would come and I would begin to pray. I had no idea when the burden would lift but I pressed in in obedience and prayed for months. I believe sometimes we miss our breakthrough because we cease praying even when the Lord has not lifted the burden of prayer from us.

Then one day as I attended the Sunday service, the pastor said he had an announcement to make. He said the reason why that church denomination came into being was to impact the community with the kingdom life within us and to have missions in every street in every city with the aim of impacting those who need to know Jesus.

The pastor said the revelation had come that we were to return to that purpose for which the church was formed and with

immediate effect that Sunday, the church was not going to exist as it was but that members were going to be split into groups to start missions in different part of communities within Lagos with the aim of seeing the missions and local churches grow, especially with those who had not known Jesus. I believe the model was to follow that of the Acts of the Apostles when *"the Lord added to their number daily those who were being saved"* (Acts 2:47).

As I sat there listening to the announcement, my heart was enlarging and expanding with joy. I could hardly contain myself at this proof of answered prayer. Indeed Isaiah 66 had proved true yet again. *"Do I bring to the moment of birth and not give delivery?"* He is faithful and if God by His Spirit moves upon us to pray through what is on His heart through prayer, be rest assured He will bring it to pass if we faint not and persevere.

I continued to listen as the pastor continued to speak. The church had been looking to buy a bigger building to contain the rapidly expanding church but the revelation brought by the Holy Spirit to the church meant that plan was shelved for what was the focus on God's heart. What might seem to be a good idea is not always a God idea, for God's ways are higher than ours. There is nothing wrong with building bigger churches if need be, but we must remember the church of God is not made with hands and the church that is on God's heart must be without walls to be able to reach to the communities with the kingdom within us.

As people's names began to be put in groups to head into different mission fields in Lagos, I found that my name had been put amongst those to minister in an area called Alagomeji. Most of us in this group were young on-fire intercessors and evangelists who were grouped under the leadership of Pastor Adeniyi Ajibola to embark on the mission to start a church called the Good Shepherd Pasture which would impact that neighbourhood.

We had little in terms of finances or buildings but we had a lot of faith which according to Scripture is tangible. Hebrews 11: 1 says faith is the evidence of things hoped for and assurance of things we do not see. A lot of things we saw happen was due to the tangibility of the faith we had.

Our team found out we had been sent to set up a church/mission in a place with lots of challenges but we were pretty excited to see what the Lord would do with the situation. What happened will encourage all who are planting and building in a hard area, with little resource other than the Holy Spirit!

Some of the challenges we encountered included witchcraft and occult practices. I remember one Saturday at the beginning of the mission, I was leading one of the teams on house to house evangelism, and as we ministered to one man, he calmly told us what type of evil Spirit he operated under and what happened when the spirit was in operation. He said it so calmly, as if it were a normal day- to-day occurrence for him! But praise God we cast out the demon from him and he became saved.

Another challenge we faced was finding a building for a place of worship. We found a place we could afford but it was an uncompleted building without doors or windows and had floors that were broken. We had to believe for the finances to finish the building but there were other situations regarding it that we also had to contend with.

The neighbours told us that the skulls and bones of dead people were buried under the building. We were told this building was under a curse and those who had tried to buy it in the past had fallen under the influence of the curse and had either gone mad or had to flee the place under strange circumstances.

So we were not only in a vicinity that was rife with works of darkness but now, the building where we were planning to establish a church was said to be under a curse! We had a meeting and decided we were going to stay in that building and do the work God had called us to do there. We had already been trained in prayer and spiritual warfare and we knew it was time to put what we had learnt into practice. We were assured that greater was The One that was within us than the one in the world.

Some of you reading this book might not be dealing with the same issues of witchcraft or occult practices in the places you have been called to bring in a harvest of souls. Your neighbourhood might be rife with gang warfare, prostitution, drugs, etc. The same principle applies. If in prayer we pull down every stronghold that stands against the gospel of Christ from being preached, we will see results in the atmosphere of heaven invading the area we live in.

We believed that since the day of John the Baptist the kingdom of heaven suffers violence and only the violent take it by force. We were determined not to falter but to take by force the area for the kingdom.

We also knew that our prayer levels had to increase to higher levels, so we started to have all-night prayer meetings, seven days a week. We were an army of God on the rise, and we decreed God's glory, presence and light in the area. We bound the power of darkness and commanded it to let go of souls in the area. In the Spirit, we pulled down the ungodly altars that had been built in the area. God has given us authority over our nations and kingdoms and he expects us to take dominion.

> *"See, today I appoint you over nations and kingdoms to uproot and tear down, to destroy and overthrow, to build and to plant"* Jeremiah 1:10.

We took authority and cast down strongholds of the enemy in the area and through prayer forbade any evil interference of the enemy regarding what he had called us to do. We prayed that the Spiritual atmosphere of the place would receive and be permeated with the glory of God.

The team also had a prayer strategy for the work involved in this mission we had been given. We prayed it would start without interference, become established and continue to grow.

As we embarked on Spiritual warfare over the area, we knew we had to call in the finances and the souls through prayer decrees. We called in every bit of the money that came in for the completion of the building. I remember how we prayed over many empty chairs, laying hands on them and decreeing they would be filled with people who would be drawn in by the presence of God.

We knew the church building was only a building, except it was saturated with the presence of God. By having many prayer sessions in the building as well as presence-filled powerful worship sessions, the building was almost being transformed into an ark of the presence of God. The finances we needed began to come in and we were able to finish the building.

We did not forget that we were sent to that community to release God's kingdom for the harvest, so we evangelized often by going into people's homes and many received Jesus and got saved with so much joy. By walking individually and corporately in the glory of God, what began to happen was that the glory of God within the church building began to attract people in. We had instances when folks would come in and express their surprise at how they got there. They described it as a pull that brought them into the church building that they could not explain.

Significant breakthroughs of healings and salvations began to happen. One was a woman who had been estranged from her husband for seven years. She still loved her husband, but he seemed not to love her anymore, but she kept hoping and believing for their reconciliation. After she heard that he was planning to marry another woman, she became totally disillusioned and took off her wedding ring.

When the leaders of the church noticed she no longer had her wedding ring on, they questioned her and discovered this story of events. The pastor of the church declared a simple prayer of restoration over her and within a very short time she testified of a great breakthrough. The estranged ex-husband who had been away for seven years came back to her door one morning. She opened the door and saw him prostrated on the floor asking for her forgiveness for all the hurt he had caused her. Overwhelmed, she forgave him and they got back together again.

It is interesting to note that once the church had taken off and was becoming established, there were prayer strategies in place for the work of God to keep growing. The prayer and intercessory group were split into two parts. One was called the fortress prayer group and I was in the other, called the watchman prayer group. We would worship and pray and often God would release visions and directions to us for the church and even warnings of the enemy plans.

When we had received strategies and directions from God, we would then pass this on to the fortress prayer group who would pray through the words and visions until these were established.

I believe this to be an amazing strategy for the church that shows us how to pray. Even when we have received a vision or direction from the Lord we do need to pray it through until it is

established. Sometimes we fail as Christians in seeing the vision the Lord has given us come to pass because we have not warred over the prophetic word given to us.

I Timothy 1:18 describes why we need to wage a good warfare with the prophetic words we have been given:

> *"Timothy, my son, I am giving you this command in keeping with the prophecies once made about you, so that by recalling them you may fight the battle."*

Many of you will have a prophetic word, or a personal word or vision regarding breakthrough in a particular area; in either the city you live in, or the place you have been called to minister in, that you will see a rich harvest of souls. Perhaps it is time to wage a good warfare using those prophetic words until those words or promises manifest and become established. That is what the Spirit of travail is there for, to help us bring forth our God-given dreams that came from the heart of God.

Cultivating an atmosphere of God's glory and presence will release miracles in every sphere of life including a harvest of souls. This could have been a very difficult church plant in many ways but it thrived for various reasons:

1. In Judges Chapter 7, the Lord showed Gideon that he needed only three hundred men in his army to win a battle. From the many thousands he had with him, the Lord showed him it was only three hundred men who he needed to win the war with the Midianites: those who were able to lap up water from the streams like a dog without kneeling down to drink. These were the most resourceful of his men who were able to press through any adversity and with these men Gideon won the war.

The team God sent to start this mission were highly resourceful young people who were very resilient to press through with the God they believed in, regardless of the circumstance. We believed the God within us was strong and mighty and we believed in the call and the mission we had been sent out to do. We expected and wanted nothing else but victory. You do not need a huge number to start a revival and we were not a huge team but God began to multiply us as His move broke forth amongst us.

2. We also knew the weapons of the flesh could not save and our war was not against flesh and blood but against demonic spirits, kings, principalities and powers in the region. Through persistent Spirit-led prayers and spiritual warfare, victory was gained in this area, which opened the area for the Spirit of breakthrough and revival to come. I remember my first visit back to The Good Shepherd Pasture Church in 2005 after I had moved to London. I went to the church address and saw the church had become so vast, with so many in attendance, that I found it difficult to find an empty seat. I was also told the church had birthed many churches and missions under it in Lagos and also other parts of the world, including the UK and Australia.

I am no longer part of this church. I was only there for about two years. Then I left for London to continue my studies, but will always remember the events that happened at this time as God trained an army of young people. These were echoes of revival carrying within it rich legacies of prayers and obedience that reverberated in so many ways because of the lessons learnt there. I could not write this book without including such a noteworthy event.

A battle which leads to victory is always won on our knees first. Heaven's attention is drawn to heartfelt, persistent and faith-filledprayers.

This chapter has shown some invaluable keys on how we need to walk into territories and gain dominion in Christ in fulfilling the great commission. Our lifestyle of faith, perseverance, obedience and prayer will go a long way to establish His kingdom here on earth.

The legacy of prayer and faith my mother taught and imparted to us has had a lot to do with my walk of faith, obedience and prayer. Her radical faith in the face of rampaging and contagious disease, where God protected us all by shielding us in his divine presence while healing those she prayed for, has instilled in me a strong belief that Jesus is master over all diseases.

This type of faith is vital for us as Christians as we have been commissioned by Jesus to minister to the sick. What do we do if we minister or start a mission where plagues or disease breaks out? While it's good to take medical precautions, the practice of living in God's secret place daily will surely cast His overshadowing presence over us and protect us from any attacking plagues.

John G Lake, the revivalist and missionary to South Africa from 1908–1913, ministered in a place where there was an outbreak of the bubonic plague which killed many, yet he was shielded from the plagues because he abided in God's secret place. He requested that the doctors placed on his hand the bubonic plague foam from the lung of a dying person. This plague died when it came in contact with him because of God's overshadowing presence in his life. It was a realm he lived in and we too can also enter into this same realm of glorious dimension here on earth (source: www.ReceiveHealing.com).

I shared earlier about how my mother's faith in prayer had caused us to be protected from armed robbers in Nigeria. I currently live in a place in London that is known for some gang

warfare. Recently, I was taking a walk at night and normally I would stop and talk to someone who I felt the Lord was leading me to. I saw two guys standing in front of their house. I stopped and said hello to them. With menacing looks, they told me in no uncertain terms, as they signalled with their hands, for me to get out of their turf.

I persevered telling them Jesus loved them. A change came on their face and they became apologetic for how they spoke and acted towards me and said they were very grateful for what I said to them. I was unafraid because carrying Jesus's presence and His love within me made me bold. When we are carried in the river of God's love, we might be led to minister to those who are leading violent lives. One thing we can be sure of is inside of them is the desire to be redeemed by their saviour. This desire is not always conscious on their part that is why they look in the wrong places, but the desire is there nonetheless and what should motivate us to step out without fear is the heartrending need for a Saviour in the heart of those who do not know Him and the reality of the overshadowing presence of Jesus that will protect us in such a situation. We should walk in this consciousness.

Concerning the move of God that took place in Lagos, I believe several factors contributed to this. The burden the Lord placed on my heart for His kingdom to be released by the believers outside of the four walls of my local church and the yielded obedience in my heart to pray through until something happened to bring God's will to earth were a definitive factors. I have a sense that others within the church were praying too and our combined walk of obedience in prayer brought a vital change in the focus of the church to be more kingdom focused within the communities outside of the church. This then led to the

dispatching of different groups to start several missions with the aim of reaching the communities with the gospel of Jesus Christ.

When our team started, the resourcefulness, faith and perseverance of the team in the face of great odds led to the move of God coming into that part of Lagos. The truth is we often have to pay a price for whatever God asks us to do. The level to which we pay the price in obedience to what the Lord is asking us to do will determine the level of how God will move within us.

We could have walked away from that difficult area and have a church plant in an easier area, but we chose to stay and pay the price by being in constant prayer, fasting and offering continual worship to God. We counted the cost and decided that Christ and what He had called us to do was worth the momentary hardship we might encounter on the way. The souls that came into contact with Jesus and received eternal life and those whose lives were touched and changed forever were very glad indeed.

The glory that God has in store for us in what He has called us to far outweighs whatever process we have to go through to get there.

> *"For our light and momentary troubles are achieving for us an eternal glory that far outweighs them all."*
>
> 2 Corinthians 4:17

The legacy of prayer imparted through my mother's life and the move of God that took place during the church plant provided echoes of revival that continue to resound until now.

Growing up in Nigeria had been a fruitful time of God preparing me for the works of revival. Moving to London began to pave the way for more of what was in God's heart for the nations. My intention was to study in England but what ensued was an

adventure that spanned across England and other nations.

Chapter Three

The River of God Continues to Flow

Whoever believes in me, as Scripture has said, rivers of living water will flow from within them. John 7: 38

A few years ago I had a dream where I was in a big flowing river. This river had a clear, silver and pure crystal colour. It was vibrant and pulsating with life with powerful currents running through it. There were other people in this river also. I noticed that the currents and waves in the river were so powerful that the currents were depositing people in different areas of different cities. Those in the river seemed to be totally submissive to its waves and were just willing to be wherever the river carried them. There were no struggles, just absolute surrender. I woke up from this dream and started to ask God what the dream meant. He told me the river was the river of revival. The purity of the river showed the absolute pure nature of the Spirit of God. The Spirit of God is holy with no contamination whatsoever and it seeks to fulfil the undiluted truth of the gospel.

The currents flowing in the river showed that the move of the Spirit was going to be so powerful that those who are fully surrendered and yielded to his Spirit will often find themselves where they are needed the most.

> *"For those who are led by the Spirit of God are the children of God".* Romans 8:14

In John 4:34, Jesus said *"My food is to do the will of Him who sent Me"* (NASB). He does nothing that He doesn't see His Father doing. How simple and how eternally true is the following scripture: *"For God so loved the world that he gave his only begotten son, that whoever believes in him shall not perish, but have everlasting life"'* John 3:16 NASB.

The very heartbeat of God pulsates with love and because He loves, He gave. In order to redeem, He sent His most precious Son, Jesus, to die for us. We all know that God is eternal and never changes. He is the same yesterday, today and forever. If it was His will to redeem souls from the beginning of eternity we can be sure He still wants to do so today.

Jesus is calling for a body of laid-down lovers who will listen to His heartbeat. His heartbeat is for souls. When we hear His heartbeat, something changes within us that makes us eternally marked for what He loves the most. Like Jesus, we will cry out and say "my meat is to do the will of Him who sent me". When we listen to His heartbeat, we become surrendered and we can flow with the tide of His river and not against it. We can flow continually in the direction of His Spirit. In this river, we can be deployed to where we are needed the most.

Being led by the Spirit of the Lord constantly in our day to day life, while ministering to those who need him the most, becomes a walk full of joy with no strife or struggle. When we are carried in the river of God to where we are needed the most for the harvest, we can release the rivers of living waters and release life to those who had been condemned to death. Jesus called us to *"shine on those living in darkness and in the shadow of death, to*

guide our feet into the path of peace" Luke 1:79.

In the following pages, I will share how being carried in the river of God has resulted in eternal life being received by so many that needed Him the most. As I share these stories, I will also highlight certain keys to revival and witnessing a harvest of souls. My prayer is that many who read this book will walk in the revelation of these keys.

In the first chapter, I talked about how I met Jesus and how He saved me. The profound experience I had in my room at that moment of salvation when I saw the presence of His light marked me forever as an evangelist - one who will live in His presence in order to release His love everywhere I go.

I witnessed a lot of souls coming to Jesus in the streets of Lagos, but moving to London about thirteen years ago made me witness an increase in the anointing that was flowing for the harvest of souls especially in an area that was not as open to the gospel.

An important key to being an effective witness is to understand that the heart of Jesus never changes regarding any individual, regardless of issues like colour or race, etc. Jeremiah 9: 24 says this about the heart of God:

> *"'But let the one who boasts boast about this: that they have the understanding to know me, that I am the Lord, who exercises kindness, justice and righteousness on earth, for in these I delight,' declares the Lord".*

This might sound very simple but when I moved to London, I became a member of a vibrant predominantly black Spirit-filled church. At the time I joined, the evangelism department was going through a crisis of disappointment regarding reaching souls in London for Jesus. One day, I went to someone from

the church's evangelism team and shared with him how much I believe Britain was going to be a harvest ground for souls. However, he had been disappointed with his efforts of trying to win the lost and he simply told me he did not want me to be disappointed too in my zeal. He said the English people were often intellectual in their beliefs and in how they perceived God and that no matter how hard he had tried to witness to them, he had not been able to get through to their heart.

He believed the Lord had given them over to judgement. That sounded like a terrible thing to pronounce but he could not see the possibility of a move of God where he had given his all to bring Christ to those he was ministering to. This is why we have to step into the Spirit in order to see the move of God in our everyday life. I told him the Lord had not given the British over to judgment and he will save them if we persevere.

With Isaiah 66: 8 ringing in my Spirit *"Can a country be born in a day or a nation be brought forth in a moment?"*, I went into my home and began to pray and the Holy Spirit began to move within me to groan and travail in the Spirit for the salvation of souls. The Lord will always answer when we seek Him with all our hearts, and within a short time as we began to go out in the streets of London, many hearts began to turn to the Lord as He poured out His Spirit through us. I remember one of the first British men I led to the Lord during our street evangelism told me to wait for a minute and then he came back with a gift of flowers thanking me for bringing him such good news! The river of God had started flowing with an outpouring of the Father's love and hearts were being changed.

I am going to share what happened around 2007 as a testament to God's goodness, and how walking by His Spirit can have such life changing and eternal consequences in the lives of people.

When we have eyes to see as the Father sees we allow Jesus to walk in our shoes without limiting Him.

Background to Brian's Story

This story is about how God changed the life of an old homeless man called Brian Cann, a man seemingly friendless and alone, but who I am confident died in Christ. I hope this testimony does his life and the immense grace of God justice, as I tell his story through the eyes of someone who God briefly placed in his path with such glorious consequences. Thank God!

As a Christian, my deep love for both God and people has motivated me to share His love and love the unsaved into His kingdom. However, I experienced an extraordinary time in my life that I can only describe as a continuous encounter with God which I walked in for several months. I cannot even describe how this happened. I woke up one morning carrying an even deeper fire of the love of God in me. As I stepped onto the streets and looked into people's eyes, I saw their souls and felt their pain. It was like Jesus was walking in me in a way I had never allowed Him to walk before.

I had encountered the perfect love that cast out all fear. I approached people on the streets who looked like they could attack unprovoked, but prompted by the Spirit of God, I felt no fear. God had found a voice and a heart to express Himself through. Many gave their lives to God. Those He touched and who gave their hearts to Him became so many that they were a sea of faces and then a blur. All I know is that I approached whoever He asked me to.

I formed a practice of leaving home early in order to speak to as many people as possible before work. My shopping trips became

extended times which stretched to hours as God delighted in speaking words of encouragement, hope and life through me. For some it took five minutes and others half hour or an hour, but they gave their hearts to Jesus. I could see the transformation from anger or disbelief to a feeling of "Can I dare to believe?" As I passed by a man one day, he cursed God with a loud voice. I stopped as the pain in his spirit pierced my heart. I walked to him boldly and in love. With God's presence with me, he soon broke down in tears as God convicted him of His love and his heart was won for Him.

One day, I had a conversation with the Holy Spirit. I said "Lord, what is happening? I feel completely undone. I have been involved in evangelism many times in the past but this visitation has left me undone." I continued, "Lord all those people who I led to Christ at this period, how am I even sure someone will follow through with them? They are too many for me to do anything about. Why does everything suddenly seem so urgent?" He did not tell me why. He just said, "In time you will understand."

One day I was on my way to Chiswick Christian Centre in London for a conference with James Maloney from America. I was looking forward to it but did not get there until it had almost finished. I could not get past the eyes of people on the way. I saw into their souls and knew them so intimately, though I had never seen them. I stopped and talked to them. Most listened, stopped what they were doing, conversed with me and opened up and gave their hearts to Christ. Even the conference I loved could not hold me back.

Brian's Story

One afternoon at work, I was introduced to Brian Cann, a man I thought I did not know. I was at work when I heard my mobile

phone ring. It was a policeman who asked me if I knew anyone named Brian. My heart started racing. I knew several as he sounded so ominous and said there had been an accident. I told him about all the Brian s I knew. He said an old homeless man named Brian Cann had been hit by a car and died. They had tried to contact his family but could not find his family. All he had was a scrap of paper with my name and phone number written on it. My heart was racing even more, as I tried to remember him and suddenly I thought about all those I loved into the kingdom.

Because there were so many during this season of my life, they had become a blur of faces as I could not remember them all, but I did remember approaching several homeless people and witnessing His love with His convincing presence. At that time, I would only give my phone number to homeless men after I led them to the Lord. Since they were too poor to have phones, the only way they could keep in touch was to have my number.

As I sat thinking, the policeman said they had searched for a month and as I was the contact person they found on the scrap of paper on him (they were unable to find his family), I had to make the decision regarding arrangements for his funeral and dates. I agreed to make this decision and said I would attend his funeral. Though I could barely remember him, I felt like a real relative.

I came off the phone feeling intensely sad. I knew he had given his life to the Lord, but the reality of his life hit me. He was seventy and had no one to love him. But one day a lady (me) smiled at him and said God loves you. He felt not only God's love but also the love of a person – something he had not felt in a long time. I was amazed. As a homeless man, wandering from place to place, he had carried a scrap of paper with my name on it for a month or two. He never lost or threw it away. I felt

humbled. And then I remembered the Holy Spirit saying to me "Soon you will understand."

The Lord began to cause me to understand the urgency of the times we are in. I understood it is not about preaching out of some religious requirement but it's about being one with The One who gave Himself and allowing ourselves to feel as He feels. What constrained Jesus to die and love the people as he did? I felt like I was walking in his shoes (well, almost).

I understood the bigger picture. God knew the end of Brian was near even when I did not. But I believe that during the last months of his life, not only did he have salvation but he dared to believe in love again. It could all have been so different for him, but thank God the one who I now remember as a friend, is resting in his Father's arms.

I went to his funeral. I sat in front of his coffin. No family was there. Though I knew he was in heaven, I wept for him; for how long he had been alone. I thought of the legacy God had for him that the thief tried to steal, and I said, "God, by a miracle will You distribute this legacy to others?" And I thought, "Brian if you are watching, you are important, deeply loved by God and myself, and one day I will see you."

Amen! For such a man indeed the world was not worthy. Let us pour out our souls for the many hungry in this world. For many in this world who are hurting or away from Christ, their stories can be re-written. Amen!!

Being led of the Spirit will oftentimes mean we are moving with the frequency of heaven, for example, being sensitive enough to connect with the Lord's heart regarding the urgency and timing of a specific person's need for salvation. Of course, we are encouraged and even commanded to preach in and out of season

which means we are free to preach the gospel to anyone even if we don't always hear from the Holy Spirit to do so because we already have a general mandate to preach, but have you ever stopped to wonder why you could be walking on the street when your eyes or spirit connect to a particular person? Why you feel such a sense of urgency in communicating the gospel to someone straight away? What draws you to a particular person?

I believe God has angels of harvest on assignment to nudge us to specific people who are right at the point of salvation or that need to receive Jesus as a matter of urgency within a time period. Hebrews 1:14 says:

> *"Are not all angels ministering Spirits sent to serve those who will inherit salvation?"*

The angels have been released on earth to serve those who are not yet saved by leading God's obedient people to them so they can be recipients of this salvation. This is what I believed happened with Brian Cann. God and the angels knew his time was near and they needed someone to communicate the gospel to him at that time.

We preach the gospel motivated by love, but if we love we must also realise that the gospel is a matter of life and death, because a decision to receive or reject Jesus could result in spending eternity in heaven or hell.

Another story of a precious lady I met buttresses this point. A few years ago, I was out shopping and I went into a restaurant in Peckham, London, to get something to eat. I noticed there were several waitresses busy serving customers, but one of them caught my attention so strongly that I felt I had to speak to her. I believe this was an inner unction of the Spirit of the Lord leading me to this particular woman. Even though she was quite

busy, I asked her if I could speak with her. She agreed to have a chat with me and sat down.

Usually I will engage someone in a conversation to get to know them and their heart before I give them a word from the Lord or share the gospel with them. But in this instance I had only a short window of opportunity so I simply told her Jesus loved her and died for her sins. I asked her if anyone had ever told her to give her life to Jesus. She told me several had spoken with her, but she had never done so. I told her I did not think she could put it off any longer. The Lord opened up her heart and she received Jesus into her heart as Lord and Saviour.

I contacted her a few times on the phone afterwards but a few months later when I went to the same restaurant and asked for her, I was told by her colleagues that she had recently taken ill with stomach problems and passed away shortly after. It was, of course, sad but I remembered the urgency with which the Holy Spirit had led me to pick her out of all the other waitresses and speak to her.

When we are flowing in the river of God, not only are we directed by Him but we can also sense the urgency and timing of heaven regarding different people. This leads us to reach out to them. He desires that all will be saved and that none will perish.

Chapter Four

Being led by the Spirit Releases Authority for a Harvest of Souls

"And my message and my preaching were not in persuasive words of wisdom, but in demonstration of the Spirit and of power, so that your faith would not rest on the wisdom of men but on the power of God". 1 Corinthians 2:4-5 NASB

Certainly one of the keys to being an effective witness for Jesus is the ability to demonstrate great authority in our witnessing for Him. We read the account in Acts 2 about how the apostles were endued with great power and boldness after the Holy Spirit came upon them. These believers were transformed into an army of bold warriors for God who preached with great authority.

In Acts 4 after Peter and John had healed the lame man in the name of Jesus, they were arrested and forbidden to speak the word of the Lord in the name of Jesus. They simply replied that they would rather obey God than man.

"But Peter and John answered and said to them, 'Whether it is right in the sight of God to give heed to you more than to God, you be the judge; for we cann stop speaking about what we have seen and heard.'" Acts 4:19-20 NASB

When we are full of the Spirit and are being led of the Spirit we can sometimes be led into circumstances where we will need

to demonstrate boldness and authority. Jesus experienced this, as did his disciples and Paul, and we as the followers of Jesus will often encounter such circumstances and opportunities to demonstrate authority also. Many are called to minister to the Muslim community and in places where it is not so easy to minister the gospel. I pray that sharing the following events will bring enlightenment and release keys in these areas.

Speakers' Corner, London 2007-2008

In 2007, a friend from a local church I was attending was visiting Speakers' Corner to preach the gospel. Speakers' Corner is a place in London where a wide variety of people gather to speak on various issues close to their heart. They have an attentive audience from many who come and listen to whatever message they feel connected to. I remember on one visit to Speakers' Corner seeing a man wearing red devil horns on his head speaking to an attentive audience! This place also had a company of radical Muslims who felt very strongly about what they believed in. The police had to be there every Sunday to contain any volatile situations that might arise.

The first time I went to see my friend who was ministering there, all around him was a large number of hecklers who seemed quite angry and were raining abuses at him. The scene looked very volatile and I was wondering how anyone would get saved in this environment as those being preached to just did not seem to listen and seemed to become increasingly angry. I went home with a troubled spirit and it just did not seem I would be back there under those circumstances.

That night I went to bed and as I slept I had a dream so vivid that it seemed real. I was standing on a ladder in Speakers' Corner preaching. As I preached, no one listened but they just heckled

and shouted. Suddenly I looked up into the sky and I saw dew come from the heavens which seemed to settle on and saturate the words I was speaking. Instantly, those very words were transformed. I would later understand that dew represented the power and authority of God because as soon as the words I was speaking had an encounter with the dew of heaven, there was a change in the atmosphere and a change in the reception that my words received. In the dream, every one became silent and listened with rapt attention to the words and all gave their lives to Jesus at the end.

I woke up with understanding and revelation deep within me that I had been called and commissioned with power to go and be a witness for Jesus in Speakers' Corner. I was excited to see where being carried in the river of God's Spirit would take me to. Initially, in my excitement I shared with a couple of my friends and invited them to come and minister with me. Their initial reception was trepidation and fear about ministering in such a volatile place. So for most of the first year, I would go on my own every Sunday.

Let me explain here that being called by the Lord and being led by the Spirit is not always easy, but when we obey the voice of the Lord, He will provide all we need, including angelic accompaniment. No one who is working with the Lord is truly alone. The most important key the Lord revealed and imparted into me was that to be completely filled with Christ is to be filled with love because "God is love".

I was to love the Muslims and everyone in that place no matter how they reacted to the gospel. Jesus loves them so completely and they would choose him if the veil that was against them listening to the gospel would be removed. As I waited on the

Lord, I became so totally possessed with His love. We must love those we minister to no matter how radical or hostile they are.

However, Jesus also teaches that we must first of all bind the strong man holding a city or person bound before we can release them.

> *" In fact, no one can enter a strong man's house without first tying him up. Then he can plunder the strong man's house"* Mark 3:27

I would often spend time worshipping and being saturated with the presence of God. We are called to be an army of love, but we are still very much an army that is in battle. Ephesians 6 talks about how to put on the full armour of God. Filled with boldness at the power in the name of Jesus and being filled with the Spirit, I would bind the strong man and command him to loose the Muslims and all the souls at Speakers' Corner. I would then pray for an army of the angelic hosts to be released ahead of me as I prepared to go to speak and minister His love.

The battle was already won beforehand in the Spirit realm so when I went to Speaker's Corner the Lord would release His presence and would give me words of power and love to speak, which convicted many Muslims to receive salvation and the love of Jesus.

Of course there was confrontation, as I found one Sunday as I stood on the ladder to speak. I was commanded by an irate man, who was a Muslim, not to proclaim Jesus as the only way. When I refused to obey him and I continued to speak, he reached out to suddenly pull the ladder from under me and instinctively I had to jump off the ladder or I might have been injured. He stood on the ladder and began to proclaim Mohammed to be lord. The Lord had given me boldness and I just simply told those who

were now listening to him that he had stolen the ladder from me. They told him to return it to me and I continued to preach as normal!

Jesus' fame will often spread when such occurrences happen and soon other Christians began to ask me how Muslims were coming to Christ in such a hard ground. I made it very clear it had nothing to do with my ability but that any life yielded to the Holy Spirit and dedicated to being filled with the love and person of Jesus, will often be called to a walk of obedience, which will result in the manifestation of the love and power of Jesus.

Several believers in the local church I was attending who were encouraged by the testimonies of Jesus moving among the Muslims and people of other faith began to go with me to Speakers' Corner. Together we would seek the Lord's presence till we became immersed in the Spirit's fire. Many more came to know the Lord but none so awesome a testimony to the power of Jesus as Sam's testimony.

Sam - a persecutor of Christians

Oftentimes when I went to Speakers' Corner I encountered a man who seemed so fearsome as he raged and screamed at Christians when they preached - especially at women preachers. He himself was not a Muslim but seemed so antagonistic to the Christian faith. For a while we never really spoke until a day came when I was there with my team. We often stood at the back of the square worshipping for a while and then I would stand on the ladder and begin to speak words of life. This went on for a while and it was amazing to see the Lord touch so many lives.

That day as I looked in front of me and watched another Christian preacher on the ladder as he debated with the Muslims

and those who listened to him. I remember thinking it was a very heated debate and the listeners became very angry as they hurled abuse at the speaker. Suddenly he looked behind and saw me and motioned for me to come and address those he was speaking to. At the time I refused, being content to remain with my team where we were saturated with the presence of God and were seeing much fruit.

However this Christian preacher did something I considered very strange at the time, but later on realised the Lord was in it. He brought the ladder from where he was and put it right in front of me and left! This meant that all the angry group of people who surrounded him now surrounded me and they now seemed very angry with me.

As I contemplated what to do, I felt the Lord nudged me to climb the ladder and speak. As I climbed the ladder, I remember feeling that I was filled with his perfect love that cast out all fear. I remember also hearing the enemy's whisper as he told me that Sam, the big, tall guy who was a persecutor of Christians and the group's ringleader, would give me a very hard time indeed. Still I pressed on allowing the Lord to release words of His Life and power through me.

As the shouts and intimidation continued, suddenly I saw Sam lift his hands signalling to and commanding his followers to be silent and listen to what I had to say. I remembered the dream I had when the dew of authority came on the words I spoke and all fell silent. They began to listen with rapt attention as words of life poured out of me and one of them remarked why no one had ever spoken like I did. I do not believe for an instance he was remarking on the eloquence of my words or on my ability but it was the Spirit's power that made all the difference.

The team continued to move around the crowd sharing the word of life when suddenly Sam came to me saying he had a request to make. I thought to myself that he had had enough and simply wanted me to be quiet but he made a request for us to sing the song 'How great is our God, The splendour of a king'. I was speechless at such a transformation in this man's heart but the Bible does say that the earnest expectation of the creatures ia awaiting the manifestation of the Sons of God (see Romans 8:19) and something in the Spirit of Sam had begun to respond to the manifestation of Christ within us.

A wonderful team member of mine named Yvonne heard this request and under the inspiration of the Spirit, she proclaimed that as soon as we finished singing the song he would give his heart to Jesus. We sang the song with all the presence and the power of Jesus within when suddenly I heard this team member scream, "Sam has given his heart to Jesus!" She had led him to the Lord. What an amazing day that was with all the hosts of heaven rejoicing.

From that day on, Sam never came to Speakers' Corner to persecute Christians anymore. I ran into him a year later and he told me he had moved to America where he had joined a Pentecostal church and he is growing in Jesus!

Amazing encounters like this will happen if we cultivate a lifestyle of living in His presence and allow ourselves to be filled in and consumed with a perfect love that casts out all fear. But remember, that we will often be called on by our Lord to demonstrate a walk of obedience to love those he died for. Jesus demonstrated the love he has for the Father by his obedience.

> *"And being found in appearance as a man, he humbled himself by becoming obedient to death-even death on a cross!"*
>
> Philippians 2:8

Our love walk with Jesus will cause us to lay down our all. It's the same love that causes us to die to self that also releases power and authority to set the captives free.

Chapter Five

Lazarus... In This Place the Dead Shall be Raised

These were the words I heard whispered in my spirit as I lay in my hotel room in Mali in November of 2007. I had just arrived in Mali with a team from my local church in London on a mission trip to bring the gospel of Jesus into this Muslim nation. The whole team was excited and full of zeal regarding what Jesus was about to accomplish but I kept feeling in my Spirit that I needed to hear a direct word from the Lord regarding this trip. Proverbs 29: 18 says without a vision the people perish, so I lay on my bed in the hotel room and waited on the Lord, worshipping, praying and interceding for the precious people of Mali.

As I waited, listening for the heartbeat of Jesus, my desire was to hear His heart for the people He created. I knew that one powerful revelation from the heart of Jesus, filled with His powerful life, was enough to set the captives free.

As I surrendered to the Lord, suddenly I heard one word breathed from the Spirit of Jesus into my spirit - 'Lazarus'. I asked the Lord what the word meant and he said 'In this place, Mali, the dead will be raised'. It was as if with that single word, He breathed faith and resurrection power into me. I knew the Lord had spoken and that Mali was going to experience newness of life in Christ.

The heart of Jesus does not change whether it be for an individual or a nation. His desire is to save all and for all to experience him in the totality of who He is - Saviour, Messiah and Redeemer.

For many of you believing for breakthrough for salvation and revival for your nation, the Lord wants you to know He has every nation in His heart. He is doing a new thing for those who will dare to believe Him wholeheartedly and who go all the way with Him in faith. Wherever He sends them, He will release accelerated harvest beyond that which you can ever think or imagine.

> *"Who has ever heard of such things? Who has ever seen things like this? Can a country be born in a day or a nation be brought forth in a moment?".* Isaiah 66:8

The Lord is saying to just ask and He will give you the nations. The fields are already ripe for harvest. He says:

> *"Ask of me and I will surely give the nations as your inheritance and the very ends of the earth as your possession".* Psalm 2: 8 NASB

This particular testimony is of God releasing supernatural breakthrough in Mali as a testament to the will and intent of Jesus. It shows what the Lord can do with each and every one who believes for the nation they are sent to. A testimony which gives glory to God, as the Almighty God of breakthrough.

As a team, we would wake up each morning and have breakfast followed by a time of prayer for each other and for the villages we were going to. This was followed by a debriefing where each team and a leader was assigned and sent to different villages to preach the gospel through crusades and evangelism. The cross was our primary message and we were to preach the gospel, heal the sick and cast out demons.

As we started the journey, simply travelling to the villages was eventful and memorable. It took about four hours to drive to each village at night and another four hours to drive back to our

hotel. Nearly every night, the vehicles we drove in would break down and we would have to stop to fix the tires.

As each team with their leader went to minister in the villages, there were reports and testimonies of salvations and healings in the villages in Mali. I remember the first village I saw as if it were yesterday. The ground was made of brown mud as the roads were not tarred yet. The villagers, men and women with kids, ran towards us and were so happy to welcome us. They even did a special dance in honour of our visit. That meeting went very well with God saving and healing so many. There were reports from other teams who also testified to the goodness of God in saving and healing many.

So far so good, but we were not aware of the situation ahead of us that would pose a spiritual contention and challenge, but God knew. Nothing takes our God by surprise. If we will walk with Him and are led by Him, He has a solution to any confrontation that might be standing as an obstacle to what He has called us to do. One night I was asked to lead one of the teams to a village to hold a crusade. With the victories Jesus had given us on the other trips still fresh in our minds, we were excited about what was ahead of us.

I think of how the Lord broke though on that trip and I pray this testimony encourages you, especially if you have been called to minister in places identified as spiritually hard ground. I also think of the number of times when I have spoken at meetings and conferences and I have seen a lot of hungry believers come forward for prayers and impartation believing for a release of revival fire that will cause the heavens to open in their area.

I want to encourage you that if you are believing for breakthrough in your region, because you have Jesus in you, you already carry an open heaven for your area. At the end of this testimony, I will

be sharing on keys on how to release the grace we carry inside to effectively bring a shift that causes the light of God to have dominion in the places we have being called to serve.

When we got to the village, we were extremely surprised and were left wondering as to why no one was at the meeting we had driven all that way for! We were met with a vast empty ground that should have been full of people expecting a touch from Jesus. Usually such a crusade would have been advertised by pastors doing missions in the different villages encouraging many to come and receive their healing and a touch from Jesus. As a result the crusade ground would usually be packed full of people and the atmosphere buzzing with excitement with the anticipation of those who had come expecting a touch from God.

So you can imagine our surprise at seeing no one except for a few pastors. The atmosphere also seemed dark and dismal and so we asked the pastors why there was no one in attendance. We were told the villagers on being told about the crusade had decided they did not want to come. The more I looked at the dark empty ground, the more I thought, 'this ought not to be so'.

I became consumed and possessed with the Spirit of faith. My faith connected to the intention of God for the souls in that place and I started to think God thoughts about the place we were in, for surely it was the Lord's will to save all and allow no one to perish and for all to come to the knowledge of the truth.

As the Lord began to pour his thoughts in my heart, I remembered the teaching of Jesus on binding the strongman first of all before spoiling his goods.

> *"Or again, how can anyone enter a strong man's house and carry off his possessions unless he first ties up the strong man?" Matthew 12:29*

Jesus was simply revealing that in areas where there is a strong opposition to the move of God, we can be effective if we can tie up or bind the strongman that is standing in opposition to his move which in this case has to do with the harvest of souls. I believe that if there was no veil on the hearts of men deceiving them from believing the truth of the gospel, a lot more people will have the freedom to choose Jesus and eternal life in heaven.

In response to the revelation, I led the team to start issuing decrees for the strongman to lose his hold on the souls of the villagers. We decreed that the hold over their souls would be loosed so that they would have the freedom to be able to choose Jesus. We kept on decreeing with earnest intercession although when we looked, we still did not see anyone coming for the crusade. We did not give up but kept on pressing in using different keys that the Bible gave us to use in prayers.

By faith, we began to call forth as sons and daughters of the living God those who have been destined to fulfil their destinies in Christ. A powerful anointing came over us as we prayed through this scripture in Isaiah 43:6:

> *"I will say to the North,' Give them up!' and to the South, 'Do not hold them back.' Bring my Sons from afar and my daughters from the end of the earth"*

We started to feel breakthrough. It was as if our very words were like hammers breaking through and we could feel the resistance shifting. We commanded the heavens to open and for revival to be released.

Suddenly I looked far away in front, people started coming out of their homes. They were coming out to attend the crusade in large numbers. The Lord had won the battle. The whole crusade ground was filled and I began to preach and speak the word

of life from the heart. The simplicity of the gospel wooed the hearts of those who listened. The Holy Spirit convicted hearts and souls of the truth of the salvation that only Jesus brings.

As the Lord led me to make the altar call, our hearts were enlarged with joy as the whole village who attended the crusade came forward gave their hearts to Jesus. With the release of the breakthrough anointing from the Lord, miracles and healings also began to happen spontaneously and many testified to healings, even getting rid of their amulets and objects they were wearing that had dark powers attached to them. They wanted to serve Jesus completely with their whole heart!

At the end of the crusade, the pastors told me it was the first time the gospel had ever been preached in the village. There had been several attempts by pastors to preach in this village but there had been no breakthrough.

Why did this move of God happen in this village in Mali?

Firstly, I believe because our faith and prayers, specifically the issuing of faith filled prophetic decrees, played a big part in the move of God here.

All through the Bible, we have stories of men of faith who through great difficulties were able to inherit the promises of God through faith. Caleb and Joshua were great men of God who were two of the twelve spies sent to spy out the land. Although the land they were sent to spy indeed had giants, these two men of faith agreed with the promise of God that they were going to possess the land and they never lost sight of that.

Hebrews 11:33 talks about those who through faith conquered kingdoms, administered justice, and gained what was promised; who shut the mouths of lions. Those looked like pretty

impossible or difficult things to do compared to what the Lord is asking us to do today but because faith brings us to the levels of the possibilities of God where all things are possible, all we need to do when faced with difficult circumstances is to choose to believe and walk out the promises which God has given to us.

Secondly, despite the circumstances we face, the Lord will give us a rhema word or revelation for our situation if we ask Him. In the case of this move that happened in the village in Mali, the word the Lord had given was regarding Lazarus (the same power that raised Lazarus from the dead will also raise to life dead situations). He was already revealing that I was going to face circumstances that looked as good as dead, but like Jesus if we would speak and call forth life into the death situation that we face, then life will indeed come forth. Those villagers who did not know Jesus were dead in their trespasses and sins but when we kept on issuing these faith filled prophetic decrees, they were able to receive the life of Jesus into their Spirit.

Next, as I mentioned earlier, for those who are crying out for an open heaven in their area or nation, who are believing God for a harvest, they already have an open heaven through the person of Jesus within them. But what releases the Lord or the Spirit of breakthrough are the decrees that we make that align with the life of God within us.

Lastly, we are not to shy away from contention or spiritual battles in situations or when we experience difficulties in the areas we are called to bring in a harvest. The truth is there is a battle in the heavenly realm from spiritual forces of darkness in regions and territories that do not want souls released to be saved.

In such situations, we can take authority by resisting the enemy, for if we submit to God and resist the enemy he will flee. We can

also bind the strongman according to the scripture quoted by Jesus in Matthew 12:29. We are also exhorted to praise God because it is also an effective weapon against spiritual adversaries.

> *"May the praise of God be in their mouths and a double edged sword in their hands, to inflict vengeance on the nations and punishment on the peoples to bind their kings with fetters, their nobles with shackles of iron, to carry out the sentence written against them. This is the glory of all the Saints".*
> Psalms 149:6-9

Right now we can ask Jesus for the nations and the ends of the earth as our possession. In every region we are in, the Spirit of breakthrough is being released and strength is breaking through for us like never before. Heaven is releasing reinforcements. Good news, friends, the Lord has won the battle and we can possess our nations for Jesus.

CHAPTER SIX

God-Given Dreams Become Reality

"And it shall come to pass afterward that I will pour out My Spirit on all flesh; your sons and your daughters shall prophesy, your old men shall dream dreams, your young men shall see visions.". Joel 2:28 NKJV

I am going to explore how listening to God and hearing him through dreams and visions can provide vital keys and direction to help us bring in the harvest of souls. This is certainly a strong key that led to the move of the harvest of souls that took place in Italy during 2009. I will share reasons why this move took place and keys to us all to walk in the reality of the harvests of souls we believe God for.

The book of Joel has always been a book that has fascinated me because I see it as a book revealing God's heart for His end time move and His never-changing intention to pour out of His Spirit upon all flesh. A lot of mighty signs and wonders foretold in the book of Joel will happen as a result of the outpouring of God's Spirit upon all flesh. Indeed we have already seen different moves of God with signs and wonders and a great harvest of souls over the decades and in different generations.

Bringing in the harvest of souls for Jesus happens as a result of our walk with the Spirit of God and our obedience in carrying

out the great commission of Jesus to preach the gospel to all nations and people. This outpouring of the Spirit of the Lord will be such that it will release such a work of the Holy Spirit's conviction that everyone who call on the name of the Lord will be saved (Joel 2:32).

There have been various outpourings of the Spirit of God throughout the ages and even in the present times. In the Acts of the Apostles we see great boldness in their ministry after they were baptized in the Spirit. They preached with great boldness and power and even the intense persecution they suffered did not diminish their fire or fervour for the Lord to fulfil the great commission. Miracles and great signs and wonders followed their ministry wherever they went.

In Acts 19: 11-12 it is recorded that:

> *"...God did extraordinary miracles through Paul, so that even handkerchiefs and aprons that had touched him were taken to those who were ill, and their illnesses were cured and the evil spirits left them".*

In the Bible and throughout the course of history, any place where there is a genuine move of God and an outpouring of the Spirit, signs follow that attest to Jesus.

I strongly believe that when we are walking by the Spirit of God, He will often speak to us through dreams and visions and in many other ways so that we can receive direction from Him. His speaking to us will also often be through the still small voice or revelations from his word.

When there is an outpouring of the Spirit of God, often there will be an increase of dreams and visions because Father God always wants to communicate with us, so we can be led by Him not only

in our day- to- day lives but in those things that are closest to his heart, such as leading the unsaved to receive Jesus as Saviour and Lord.

God does not leave us without a vision and oftentimes He will communicate with our spirit so we know exactly where He wants us to be and where we are needed the most. Oftentimes there is a need to hear heaven's heart for strategies to bring in the harvest of souls in certain nations.

We will certainly be more effective in expanding the kingdom of Jesus if we could hear His heart for every situation. In Acts 16: 9, during the night Paul had a vision of a man of Macedonia standing and begging him 'Come over to Macedonia and help us'. There was a change of direction for Paul who was planning to go to Asia before as he knew he had to immediately go Macedonia to help release the gospel.

It's harvest time - Italy 2009

I have already shared about the vision of the river where believers were been carried by the tides of the river to places where they were needed the most at certain times. I believe God hears the cries of the hearts in the nations and He's stirring up the hearts of believers through dreams and visions to answer this urgent heart cry.

This happened in Italy in 2009, because of a clear direction in a dream God gave me. This could happen for anyone who is obedient to the leading of the Lord in any given situation. He hears the heart cry of the nations and He made the nations and its inhabitants. Surely He has the key and divine strategies that will cause the heart of all men to open to Him. Let us press in today and ask God for the keys and direction that we need for this very important end harvest of the nations!

In March 2009, I ministered in several revival meetings in some churches in Italy. As usual, the Lord was faithful in demonstrating his great power and might in the different meetings. God's fiery presence was imparted to the believers that ignited a hunger in them to receive more of God. There were several salvations in the revival meetings and prophetic words encouraged many because they were so accurate and brought comfort and joy to many. Several lukewarm believers became much more on fire for God.

In Caserta, where I had previously ministered at a church named Chiesa Cristiana Evangelica Ecclesia, I was invited to come back by Pastor Narducci Biagio to hold another meeting at this church. I was expectant at what the Lord would do, but at the same time I was keen to find out from the Lord exactly what form He wanted the meeting to take.

I believed that if I heard from God and obeyed what He said then much needed breakthrough for Italy would be released. The practice of pressing into the presence of the Lord to see what He is requiring of us should never be lost. In the Bible, David knew this very well and he would press into the presence of God seeking and asking His heart for decisions before he would even go ahead. I believe this is why he was called a man after God's heart!

A key to revival and a harvest of souls for Jesus is for us to abide in the secret place of God's heart so we can hear what He has to say. He longs to share keys and strategies that we never know are even possible, but with Him all things are possible.

As I remained in prayer, I fell asleep and I had a dream so vivid that it seemed to be such a reality that when I woke up I was extremely surprised that it was a dream. In the dream, I was

standing in the centre of a square somewhere in Italy, preaching the gospel as a number of people surrounded me.

After speaking, I was surprised when people asked to give their lives to Jesus even though I had not even made an altar call! I woke up from this dream which had seemed so real but I knew several things had been imparted by the Lord into my spirit.

Firstly I knew beyond any shadow of a doubt that the Lord had given me a strategy for Italy - He wanted me to do a crusade in Italy.

Secondly, the night vision I had made me feel I had been impregnated with a purpose from the Lord that could not be shaken off. I had received an impartation from the Lord that would bring a harvest of souls. I therefore rejoiced and the Spirit of boldness increased upon my life.

Thirdly, I realised that the key to being successful in Italy was doing what the Lord had shown me. I felt the footprints of the Lord had gone ahead of me in Italy giving me clear directions of where to put my feet to follow Him. There is no better way to be led by the Spirit of the Lord than to seek His heart and follow Him exactly as directed. Hebrews 8:5 talks about Moses being asked to build the tabernacle according to the patterns he saw on the mountain.

There is no time in heaven in terms of beginning and end, just the vast limitless eternity. In the reality of eternity that Christ lives in, He had already gone ahead into the future to accomplish everything that needed to be accomplished in Italy. I understood that when I obeyed Him and stepped into His finished work for that particular trip.

I was so excited about God's strategy for the crusade which He had shown me, that I soon picked up the phone to speak to a

pastor friend who had several churches in Italy under his care. (This was not the pastor who had invited me) I do not remember ever telling him the dream but I did remember excitedly telling him I was planning on coming to Italy to do a crusade.

At that time I knew little or nothing about the spiritual climate of Italy, nor was I overly concerned as to ask if the climate of the nation was hot or cold for Jesus. I believed the fire of the Lord was enough to melt any heart no matter how cold.

However, when I discussed what I was planning to do, my pastor friend with well-meaning intentions told me that my plans would not work. He believed that open air crusades from his experience would normally work in fairly impoverished countries such as Asia or Africa where people are incredibly desperate for God. He told me the people of Italy were in comparison a wealthy nation and intellectual too who would therefore not respond to a crusade type situation. He said I should try another strategy that would endear the gospel to them more.

After listening to his advice, I still had no doubt at all as to what the Lord had asked me to do. When you are impregnated with an idea from the Lord or a vision, you cannot shake it off as it has become a part of you and you can only find relief when you have released or brought forth what has been given to you from the Lord.

Here is a word of caution - when the Lord gives you a dream or vision, by all means share it with those you are accountable to, but your decision to fulfil God's heart or vision rests with you. Your leader or friend might not always see things the way God has given it to you. It does not mean they do not have your interests at heart, it just means God has not communicated the

vision to them the same way he has to you.

I knew I had been given an unshakable mandate from God which had to be fulfilled the way He had given it to me. If He shows me clearly ordered steps in a vision, then it means He has already gone ahead of me and He is waiting for me at a future time in place to catch up with Him in what He has already done. He is God, who calls even the end from the beginning.

As I remained in communion with the Lord, I began to gain more understanding of how the dream was to become reality. I had usually done revival and crusade meetings to fulfil my call as an evangelist to bring the lost to the Lord, but somehow with the dream I had, I felt that training the church in Spirit-led evangelism would have a link to what I saw in the dream. That was the first time I had given formal training in a church for evangelism.

I am so thankful to the church who invited me who gave me such a free rein to do the meetings as the Lord directed me. I started the ministry at Chiesa Cristiana Evangelica Ecclesia on August 23, 2009 with a training school on prophetic and power evangelism. We studied John 4 and saw how Jesus shared God's heart with the woman by the well. He knew He had the wells of living waters but was patient enough to draw her out in a conversation, where her insecurities and walls which had been built up because of her experience of being a Samaritan were exposed, before He released the word He had for her.

I shared that ultimately the aim of revealing the Father's heart to the unsaved or demonstrating His power to heal them is to bring them to embrace the cross in salvation. At the end I prayed a prayer of impartation to release the boldness and the power of Jesus to everyone who desired to move in more of God's boldness, power and love.

When God gives a dream or vision, we should be confident enough in what the Father has said to us or shown us He will do. So all through the meeting I was waiting in eager expectation to see how the Lord would work things out.

At the end I asked the pastor where he thought we could go and minister the love of Jesus with the fresh impartation that had just been received from heaven. The pastor looked at me and said "There is a square in Caserta we can go to."

I remembered the dream I had of speaking at a crusade in a square in Italy. I knew the events were working out just as the Father had given me in a dream, so I agreed that we should go to the square.

It is a wonderful thing to see a pastor so involved with the whole vision, as well as his congregation. We got to the square as it was almost getting dark, but I noticed that rather than the people leaving to go home, they were sitting there waiting with no apparent activities going on. It struck me that somehow they were waiting for us. I remembered Romans 8: 19:

> *"The creation waits in eager expectation for the sons of God to be revealed".*

When Jesus gave me that vision of a future time in Italy where the harvest of souls was going to take place, I believe He left at the square a weight of His glory and His presence for us and those waiting to enter into. In God's timing, all the activities of that night had already taken place. He was just waiting for us to enter in and take possession of what He had already done. When the whole of creation waits and groans with eager longing for the revealing of the sons of God, they are in essence waiting for those who will reveal Jesus and His presence. They were waiting

for those who would reveal the face of Jesus to them in all His kindness, love and power. So in essence, they were waiting for us!

As we entered the square, we felt the weight of the glory of God in the square. I remember thinking there was more glory than I had encountered in some church meetings! The worship team led by Stefania Narducci, the pastor's daughter (an extremely passionate and sincere woman of God) and the youth group from the church started that night with such a powerful time of worship that we felt an increase in the presence of God. When the worship finished, I knew it was time to release the unction the Lord had given me to speak. His weighty presence and the eager expectation of His creation who were waiting in the square, were all the confirmation I needed that the Lord was about to release His word through me that would bring in the harvest.

I signalled to one of the Italian team to stand with me to interpret the words I was about to share from my heart about the beautiful gospel of our Lord Jesus Christ. We had not planned for a crusade as I had just been waiting for God to bring the dream to pass, but the Lord himself had already planned ahead of time by preparing masses of people who were already waiting with eager expectation.

I started to speak and the Lord began to share through me the words that would woo the Italian people from the heart. His cross covered with blood and His body broken with pain, were because of His love for them and for all humanity. Words of knowledge began to flow through me automatically. I was lost in Him at those moments as I spoke as the Spirit gave utterance. I believe this work of the Harvest must be a move of the Spirit from beginning to end in order for us to experience and enter into the great harvest the Lord has for us.

I continued to speak when I noticed two Italian men standing in front of me. They began to speak and my interpreter said that one of the men had come forward (though I had not made an altar call) saying he was the person who the words of knowledge applied to. He said he was the one with the sleepless nights, with terrible problems that he needed deliverance from and asked if we could pray for him. I remembered the dream when people had come forward to present themselves to receive Jesus even without an altar call being made!

I explained to the Italian men that we ourselves could not help him but that only the Lord could, but that we would pray for him in the name of Jesus to be delivered and receive freedom from his torment. He had tears in his eyes as we prayed for him. Afterwards, I asked them if they would like to give their hearts to Jesus. They said yes and invited the Lord Jesus into their hearts. It was a profound moment to see hope and restoration given to a man who had been so broken without Jesus.

The Italian team were on fire for the Lord that night as they began to mingle around the crowds speaking words of life and healing to many. The atmosphere was so open that the word of God penetrated with ease into hearts to bring conviction, hope and salvation to many.

Soon, one of the team asked me to come and pray for a woman sitting on one of the benches. As we began to speak to her, she described how her life had been full of various mishaps for a very long time and how she was now suffering from leukemia. It was very emotional for us too as we listened but we knew the Lord very much loved her and wanted to reach out to her.

We shared Jesus with her as the Lord who wanted to heal and save her and who also wanted to release joy into her heart. As

we prayed for her to be healed, I felt such heat of the presence of the Lord being released that I felt sure He was working in her body to release healing to her. As we led her to the Lord, we watched her face transform from misery and pain to utter joy. Her husband who was standing by walked away from the scene.

Later on, one of the team who spoke to him explained to us that he had walked away because he was choked with such emotion which he could not contain as he saw his wife's face happy and smiling for the first time in many years. He thanked us for bringing such joy into his wife's life. When Jesus releases such a marked transformation in the lives of people, it brings encouragement in so many ways and the host church was encouraged.

Several decisions were made that night by the church which I felt through a leading of the Lord. Through the move of the Spirit which they saw that night, they understood and received the revelation that the church was meant to go beyond the four walls of the building into the community, the highways and the byways in order to reach those in darkness who need the Lord the most.

They decided to start house meetings where unsaved neighbours would be invited as part of the ways to reach their community. They also decided for that season to have one of their church nights on a Thursday in the different city squares where the unsaved would gather rather than in the church building.

In one of the house fellowships as we gathered to worship and share the word, we noticed a girl riding by on a motorcycle stop outside of the building compound where we were holding the meeting. We later found out she had come to pick up someone who was at the meeting but she was not expecting to experience what she saw that night and unsure of what to do she stood in front of the building compound for a long while just staring at us.

The presence of the Lord that had been strong throughout all my ministry time in Italy was extremely strong that night and the power of the Holy Spirit led her in and convicted her to receive His words in her heart. We rejoiced as she gave her heart to the Lord.

In conjunction with these outreaches, I continued to hold several church revival meetings where the believers were being set more and more on fire for the Lord. It was glorious to see this transformation taking place! The Lord's heart is to raise up an army of his love and power to release revival everywhere we go.

At the last outreach we went to the centre of town mainly with the youth this time. They were amazing and very creative. They did some sketches and dramas that depicted the delivering power of Christ. I also spoke in an open square witnessing very many people raising up their hands openly to welcome Jesus as Saviour in their hearts.

Afterwards they shared their testimonies and addressed the crowd. I gave glory to God because two of the young evangelists who ministered with us were those who had given their lives earlier when I visited the Italian church in March 2009 and they remained on fire for God. I ended the meeting by sharing the gospel and inviting those who wanted to know Jesus. About twenty people responded to Jesus that night.

This testimony of what the Lord did in Italy holds several important keys for us who believe for a harvest of the lost.

You might be a normal, regular person looking for the Lord to use you in your community, in your street or various outreaches, in your schools or at work. You might be a missionary or an itinerant minister with a heart to reach the lost for Jesus. The principles the Lord revealed in Italy will be the same for you as

you press in to believe God for a harvest of souls wherever you are.

Why do I believe this move of God took place?

Firstly, the heart of the Father is always to save all and for none to perish. Jesus would still have come to die for sins even if it was only for one person! That's the extent of His love for us and shows the extent to which each and every soul is so precious to Him.

Because we are his creation and all nations are made by Him, He is well acquainted with our hearts. He knows how to open hearts and knows how He wants to release revival in every place. Above all the Lord has the power to turn the heart of nations and all to Him if only we can follow the leading of the Spirit.

The Italian people were not too academic or too wealthy or too comfortable to need Him, or to respond to the move of His Spirit in a crusade environment. He made us all and there is a vacuum in each heart that can only be filled with Him and nothing else.

It is the overwhelming conviction of the Holy Spirit and His presence the world needs. When we walk with God and we flow with His Spirit at every point, His presence will flow through as we witness to the unsaved.

Secondly, whether it is through a crusade or a drama, the release of the presence of the Holy Spirit is what will convict souls.

John 16: 8 says:

> *"When he comes, he will convict the world concerning sin and righteousness and judgment."* (NASB)

> It is not a method that brings souls to Jesus. It is His convicting presence which flows especially when we live a life that is full of the Spirit of God.

Thirdly, I believe that the ministry of Jesus on earth was so successful because He would only do what He saw the Father doing. He did not walk independently of His Father. He was God Himself but knew the secret to fulfilling His earthly ministry successfully was to look in and listen to what the Father was doing at all times so that He could step into the pre-ordered footsteps the Father had laid for Him.

The Bible tells us Jesus would go up to the mountains to pray all night and commune with His father. I believe it was during these times that He would often see and hear God's heart for the events of the coming days, making it easy for Him minister in what the Father had already shown Him. Sometimes in healing the sick, Jesus would rebuke a demon of infirmity and sometimes He just issued a command to rise up and walk. When healing a blind man in Matthew Chapter 8, He spit into a man's eyes before this man began to see!

Through the ministry in Italy, the Lord had shown me what was to take place in a dream and in Mali it was through a revelation at a time of deep prayer and waiting on the Lord. In whatever way the Lord speaks to us, what is important is to rely on Him completely and trust Him to bring to pass what He has shown us. When we are sure we have received from the Lord we must keep praying into the events He has shown us so what is already released in heaven, will manifest on earth.

The next key is obedience. It is vital to how we see God move in the harvest He is calling us to bring in. When we receive a vision

from Him, we must move to obey what He has commanded us to do.

> *"Write down the revelation and make it plain upon tablets so that a herald may run with it. For the revelation awaits an appointed time; it speaks of the end and will not prove false. Though it linger, wait for it; it will certainly come and will not delay".* Habakkuk 2: 2-3

Sometimes our obedience will be tested. The well-meaning pastor in Italy advised me that the strategy of holding a crusade in Italy would not be successful for various reasons, but it was still left to me to either obey the vision of the Lord or be swayed by the advice of man.

Faith was a very important ingredient to this move of God in Italy. We must believe what God has shown us even if we do not yet see it. I had faith against all odds to believe God would bring the vision He showed me to come to pass even though I had not seen it happen. I believed against all odds that with God nothing was impossible even after being advised otherwise about the wisdom of doing a crusade in Italy.

This is why Noah was commended in the scriptures for being a man of faith. Hebrews 11:7 says that when Noah was warned about things not yet seen, in holy fear he built an ark to save his family.

Finally, the most important reason and key for what happened in Italy, is what I believe to be the faithfulness of Jesus Himself. His heart has been faithful from the beginning to seek and save the lost. We can trust in His faithfulness to bring to pass whatever promises He has made to us regarding the harvest of souls He so clearly loves. We can trust Him to be faithful to bring to pass clear cut directions and visions He, Himself, has revealed to

us regarding what He wants to bring to pass in our cities and nations. Numbers 23:19 tells us why we can never lose when we obey Him because He is so faithful:

> *"God is not a man, that he should lie, nor a son of a man, that he should repent."* NASB

In obeying Jesus who in the realm of eternity was already in the future realm where the crusade was going to take place, I stepped into the finished work of what He had already done. We must walk and partner with the Lord to see the manifestation of the harvest we believe for. We must dream with Him and believe Him with all of our being to release what He has for our community and nation. This is the walk in the Spirit that the Lord is calling us into at this time."

Chapter Seven

A Spontaneous Move of the Spirit of God

CHAPTER SEVEN

"Surely the islands look to me; in the lead are the ships of Tarshish, bringing your children from afar, with their silver and gold, to the honour of the Lord your God, the Holy one of Israel, for he has endowed you with splendour" Isaiah 60:9

Throughout history we have seen and continue to see that God's intent, heart and purpose for peoples, nations and cities never change. From the beginning of creation, we see God creating, life, light and order in a chaotic world that had no form and was dark and void. It says in Genesis 1 that the earth was formless and void, darkness was over the surface of the deep but even in this deeply chaotic condition, the Spirit of the Lord was still moving upon the surface of the waters.

Now we see in Genesis 1:3, God commanding there to be light and there came light. In the ensuing verse, we see God separating the darkness from the light by calling the light day and the darkness night.

God knew that the key to creation was to speak faith-filled words in the atmosphere of His Spirit and glory. By His command and in the presence of His Spirit, a beautiful world was created – vegetation of every kind, livestock, creatures and animals , all created by His spoken words. The planets were made and the

stars were put into place. In Genesis 1:25, it says God looked at what He had created and He saw... it was good.

Man was His crowning glory. He created Adam and Eve and they were perfect. He was pleased to give them dominion over all the works of His hand. He soon gave Adam a warning, however. Knowing that the key to keeping darkness and sin from the beautiful world He had created was obedience, He warned Adam not to eat of the tree of the knowledge of good and evil for he would die on the day he did so.

Satan came in the form of a serpent and tempted Eve who soon gave in and gave the fruit of the knowledge of good and evil to her husband. As they gave in to temptation, they soon both realised they were naked. Sin entered them and their nature was darkened. The god of this world, Satan, got his leverage to bring darkness, sin and destruction into the world we live in. All kinds of sin including murder, envy, jealousy, strife, idol worship became rife.

The world needed a saviour and Jesus, the perfect and sinless candidate, was sent to die for the sins of this world. Whilst Adam's disobedience brought darkness and death, Jesus' obedience brought life, righteousness and salvation to all who believed in Him.

Haiti 2010

Why have I delved into the background of how sin and darkness came into the world? It is to shed some light into the events in Haiti during 2010 that brought so much carnage and destruction. Most of us heard about the earthquake that happened in early January, and by January 24th had resulted in the death of an estimated 316,000 people, with 300,000 homes damaged and one million people rendered homeless. (Source: 'Wikipedia, The Free Encyclopaedia').

What a picture of terrible tragedy of what happens when darkness is prevalent in a place and Haiti was no different to all the places where darkness had entered. Our obedience to walk with Jesus to bring life to souls in such places will always bring a transformation of His light into these places. Soon many aid services were sent to Haiti by various churches, and revival meetings were held in many areas of the country.

This was the background to the journey that was orchestrated by God into an area of Haiti which brought a beautiful move of God. I had no idea what the Lord was going to do. There was no dream or vision as in the other testimonies as to what the Lord was going to do, but if you are walking by the Spirit of God, He will lead and guide you, for as many as are led by the Spirit of God are the sons of God. Flowing and walking in the river of God also ensures that the Spirit leads us where we are needed the most.

My trip to Haiti began in an uneventful way. I rarely take holiday vacations as I usually use all my spare time to travel on ministry trips. In 2010, a ministry cruise was advertised where several speakers were going to be speaking. It was not mandatory to attend these conferences and there was a choice for it to be a holiday if that was what we wanted. The cruise was on a ship called Freedom of the Seas which in itself was a huge breath-taking work of art with a large expanse inside that made it difficult to believe it was a ship!

It was full of fun events to do - there were ice shows and various musical shows. Formal nights often took place in their 5 star restaurants where men were garbed in formal attire and women graced the tables with their lovely evening wear. It was an exotic holiday in every way. The ship also promised various excursions and trips into various islands. I felt like Alice in Wonderland

and I hardly knew what to do to contain myself on such a rare occasion of having a holiday.

As with all other testimonies I have shared, the aim is to show the exciting adventures that await us when we dare to fully immerse ourselves in the river of His Spirit where we give Him the freedom to take us and use us wherever and whenever He needs us the most. A life lived in the Spirit is an exciting one as it gives Jesus the opportunity to do what He does the most with the souls and lives He loves so much. What a privilege to daily walk with the King of Kings and the Lord of Lords!

In sharing these stories, I give all the glory to God as we are merely purified earthen vessels when we allow Him to use us at His will. As we share keys that were prevalent in allowing the move of God to break into these different places, we encourage others to press into revival in the areas they minister, so that together we can all experience a great harvest of souls to quicken the coming of our Lord and to bring much needed light into areas that have been plagued by darkness.

On the day when one of the formal nights was going to be held on the cruise, I was in the room I shared with another lady, Wendi Jones, with whom I had become friends even before the cruise. She excitedly began to plan for the night event and what she was going to wear. For some reason, I just felt led to lie on my bed praying quietly with the bed covers drawn over me. My friend asked me when I was going to get up to start preparing for the dinner event. She did not want me to miss dinner. Bless her! I must have mumbled 'soon' and soon after I heard her leave the room.

After she left, the rumbling of the Spirit of God within me seemed to get louder and the stirring more intense. As I had started

praying quietly, my plan was just to pray for a while before going downstairs for dinner but it seemed the Lord had other plans and I just did not feel released by the Holy Spirit.

The intensity of the intercession increased and I needed not to wonder what I needed to pray about because the Holy Spirit soon came alongside me to help me in prayer, in the same way the Spirit helps us in our weakness. We do not know what to pray for, but the Spirit Himself intercedes for us with groans that words cannot express (Romans 8: 26) As I prayed, the Holy Spirit began to form words in my Spirit and one of the words I heard in my Spirit and was audibly uttered were the words "Break the voodoo spells."

In obedience to what I heard the Lord say, I began to break all voodoo spells and release the presence of God wherever the spells might have taken place. We should always trust God and obey Him when we hear such instructions because there is a good reason for every act of obedience He desires from us. Events that would unfold the next day in Haiti would explain why, but at that moment I just obeyed as I prayed.

Soon, I heard the Lord speak other words into my Spirit. I heard him say 'The isles are waiting for me'. This is in reference to the Isaiah 60 scripture I quoted at the beginning of this chapter. I began to have a real sense that the prayers, decrees and intercessions I was being led to do, had to do with the island we were going to dock at the following day. The island was Haiti!

The islands were looking to the Lord and waiting for Him. He alone is the only hope to remove the darkness that had pervaded the nations and hearts of men and Haiti had certainly had its fair share of pain, tumult and darkness. I kept praying without having a clear insight to what was going to happen the next day but kept praying until I felt a release in my spirit.

When the Lord places such a burden of prayer upon us, it is good to trust in the leading of the Holy Spirit on how we pray and to be sensitive to pray until He releases this burden. That is when the breakthrough comes.

By the time I finished praying, the formal dinner event had ended and I had missed dinner. We must always give the Lord free rein to break into our agenda whenever He wants to because He is our Lord and so He can guide us in the paths of destiny.

> *"to shine on those living in darkness and in the shadow of death, to guide our feet into the path of peace".* Luke 1:79

The Lord wants to use us to shine on those living in darkness so that they can experience freedom in Christ.

Before creation, the whole world was in darkness and in utter chaos before the Father spoke His creative word that released light and order into the world and all of creation was established by His spoken word. We must be obedient and allow the Lord to lead us to those who need Him the most – the ones who are sitting in the valley of the shadow of death – to bring healing, light and illumination to them.

Isaiah 9: 2 talks about a people living in darkness seeing a great light. That prophecy was fulfilled at the coming of Jesus but in these days, we are the ones the world is waiting for to release them from darkness into light. The world wants to see the great light within us as they did through Christ. Herein is the triumph of the cross, when the light and glory of God is allowed a release without hindrance and salvation, deliverance and freedom is experienced.

The next morning we docked at Haiti. I had arranged to meet two of my other friends on the ship to tour the islands together so we could discover what fun stuff we could do. There were

opportunities to swim, to snorkel, experience several other adventures or just to lie on the beach or shop for unique gifts to take back home.

My friends and I walked around on the island for a while deliberating and chatting about what we might want to do. We decided to visit the Haiti market. This was a huge market with lots of shops both upstairs and downstairs. Activities were very busy as many tourists on the cruise from different countries visited the variety of shops to see what they could buy. For many of the Haitians who had experienced recent devastation, this was certainly a lucrative way for them to make money from the many tourists who were very eager and willing to spend their cash to buy various products on offer. There were shops selling hats, clothes and various other items. It was interesting to see that many shops also sold various ornaments or items that were usually identified with occult powers.

We chatted with a few of the shop owners and bought a few items such as large brimmed straw hats. We were planning to move on when suddenly I started to feel a nudge in my spirit. The Lord began to nudge my spirit and I felt the unction was to speak words of life in the thriving and bustling Haiti market. I specifically felt led to start an impromptu and spontaneous open air crusade and speak to those in the Haiti market about the gospel of Jesus.

I approached my two friends and told them I felt a stirring of the Lord inside me to speak His words to those in the market. I had wanted to see if we could do the ministry together but one of my friends remarked that she could not feel such a stirring. It could have been the pervasive feeling of darkness in the place that they felt. Sometimes this can overwhelm even well-meaning Christians, but we have to remember that we are called to be salt and light.

We are called to be more aware of the light and authority that we carry than we are of the darkness surrounding us. It is this confidence in the power of Christ that will cause us to be victorious even in a place of deepest darkness so that we can bring in the greatest harvest for Jesus at these times. It later turned out that my friends were also feeling the intense heat and were not feeling that comfortable about doing ministry, so they decided to move on to continue with their day's activities.

I stood still for a minute pondering what to do but I could feel the unction in me to speak increasing rather than dying out. No wonder 2 Peter 1:21 says:

> *" For no prophecy was ever made by an act of human will, but men moved by the Holy Spirit spoke from God".* *(NASB)*

In these times that we live in, we must ensure we yield to the movement of the Holy Spirit to speak as He guides, inspires or leads us, because such obedience will bring great rewards for His kingdom.

> *"But if I say, "I will not mention his word or speak any more in his name," his word is in my heart like a fire, a fire shut up in my bones. I am weary of holding it in; indeed, I cannot".*
>
> Jeremiah 20:9

Many times, moving with the direction of the Holy Spirit will call us to be resourceful. So with no team or an interpreter, I decided to approach one of the shop owners. I spoke to him and discovered he was a Christian. I told him I was thinking of doing a crusade right there in the middle of the Haiti market grounds and asked what he thought. He said he thought it was a great idea. I asked if he could interpret for me as I discovered that many there spoke other languages. He agreed and my Spirit rejoiced as I could see that heaven was providing for my needs for the task ahead.

I now had all the ingredients needed for an open air Holy Ghost crusade as heaven had provided. Willingness on the part of the team one works with is important as Psalms 110:3 tells us that God's people will be willing in the days of His power. There were masses of people in this thriving market to preach to and I was willing to trust God that He would draw the people to Him.

I trusted Him because the Lord had already told me the previous day in prayer that the islands were waiting for Him and I knew that if He is lifted up He will draw all men to Him. It is our job to be obedient and when we are obedient, we must trust in Him to do the rest because He is able. I also had a powerful ingredient which was the holy unction to speak His word and the presence of the Holy Spirit I felt within me.

> *"The power of the Lord was with Jesus to heal those who were ill".*
>
> Luke 5:17

Hallelujah, the Lord was ready! I stood at the centre of the Haiti market and began to speak words of life as Jesus gave me utterance. The message was very simple but Jesus did not disappoint in releasing His manifest powerful presence and the Holy Spirit did not disappoint in releasing His convicting power. I spoke about the light of Jesus breaking into a place that had being devastated by darkness. I spoke about the great love of Jesus and I spoke about the cross. The cross was the ultimate place of sacrifice. If they would embrace the cross and embrace Jesus for the remittance of their sins, they would receive an exchange of destiny - darkness for light!

As I shared about Jesus releasing light to break into their world, I encouraged the Haitians to make a decision to repent and renounce the unfruitful works of darkness and to even get rid of

any occult amulets they had in their possession. From the very beginning as I began to speak, the Lord by his Spirit brought many from the market to surround me and listen to the words of the gospel being spoken. Only the conviction of the Holy Spirit could be so powerful as to draw many shop owners from the very important task of making money within a limited time to leave their shops and potential customers to listen to the words of Jesus.

The people were drawn to the presence of Jesus just as people were drawn to follow Jesus when He was on earth. There is a vacuum in the heart of man that only Jesus can fill and I am so thankful the Lord made them aware of the poverty of their spirit which was more urgent than their situation. According to Matthew 16:26, what does it profit a man if he gains the whole world but loses his soul?

It was decision time! As I finished speaking, I made an altar call for those who would like to respond to Jesus to give their hearts to Him. Hands came up all over the place from those I could see who surrounded me. They were willing to make decisions for Jesus and through prayer, they confessed their sins and repented and invited Jesus into their hearts and lives to be their Lord and Saviour. What a glorious moment in heaven as the angels must have rejoiced and danced as each saint's name was written in the Book of Life.

I began to get words of knowledge from the Lord regarding various sicknesses, pains and conditions. Usually, I get words of knowledge by feeling the burning fire of the Lord on areas of my body where the sick person might be experiencing an infirmity. As I began to call out specific words of knowledge, hands came up to acknowledge the conditions were present. I prayed and

released the healing power of the Lord to break into every area of their bodies that was experiencing sicknesses and for them to be healed.

When the power of Jesus is present to heal, healing takes place and soon many were testing their bodies to see if their pains and sicknesses were gone. To the glory of Jesus, many testified that pains and sicknesses had left their bodies. Although it is the enemy's job to steal, kill and destroy, Jesus is more than capable of destroying the enemy's works and to bring life and life more abundantly and this is what He did to His glory that day.

News of this spontaneous move of Jesus began to spread around the market and soon other sections of the market that were too far out to be reached by the initial crusade outreach began to come and ask me to do crusade outreaches in different market sections too. Salvations and healings began to break out in different areas of the market as the crusade outreach continued.

I remember after doing a number of these crusade outreaches and I was somewhat tired physically (after all it was a blazing hot day too), another man asked me to come to another section of the market to do another crusade outreach because the need was so great. I remember remarking that I was tired and I laugh till this day when I remembered his response. He told me, 'You cannot be tired because we need this here'. Their hearts and spirits were so enlarged by what the Lord was doing that they could not get enough and so I continued. Jesus was still in the business of winning souls, so I continued in the journey with Him.

After one of the sessions of the crusade ministry, I looked and saw a number of people coming from the boat into the Haiti market and I recognized them as some of the Christians we were

with on the ship. Wendi Jones, my friend and cabin mate, was also among those just alighting from the ship. I walked up to them and told them about what the Lord had been doing in the market and about the wonderful work of healings and salvations that had been taking place. I asked them if they would like to be part of this and help as the need was still so great and many still needed a touch from God especially in the area of deliverance and receiving freedom.

They said yes, they would love to be part of the ministry in the Haiti market. I had another confirmation that the Lord always provides when we are obedient to Him. He had provided a ministry team and I was grateful.

We had a simple strategy. I continued with the public crusade speaking while the team moved amongst the people praying individually for each person's needs. Whatever their needs were, they were prayed for. Sicknesses were prayed for and some who were backslidden were led in prayers of repentance. Some started to remove their amulets deciding to trust in God alone. Businesses were also prayed for to prosper. Many of the Haitians had lost their businesses as a result of the earthquake but our God is a good God who desires that His children prosper even as their souls prosper.

This was such a great time of freedom being experienced in every way that we gave God all the glory. Souls were saved, bodies were healed, demons were cast out and many lives restored. This is what happens when we make a decision to go about our Father's business.

When we are carried in the rivers of His Spirit, indeed we never know where His Spirit will lead us, but we can be sure it will be a blessing to those who need Jesus so desperately.

In closing, I will share what I believe to be the keys to why this move of God in the Haiti market place took place.

1. The first key is sensitivity in being prepared by God in whatever area He wants to use us, even if we do not know exactly what He wants us to do. There were key preparations that needed to take place before the Haiti event. The day before, I had the urgency of the prayer need the Lord had placed on me. The thought of sitting through the second formal night was very attractive so again it is worth noting that we are called to carry our cross daily even when it is not convenient! Being sensitive to the Holy Spirit for another person might be to be called to a fast especially on a day when the person is very hungry. Such a simple act of obedience can make a lot of difference.

   When we wait on the Lord and are sensitive to hear what He has to say, He will give clear instructions because He does not want to leave His people without a vision. The first word I heard clearly in the place of prayer was firstly to break the voodoo spells. It was very clear that certain spells and curses over that area had needed to be broken to clear the atmosphere for the following day's ministry in order for there not be any hindrance to the move of God.

   The second word I heard was that the isles were waiting for God. This gave me a hint that the prayers I was being led to pray had to do with docking in Haiti the next day. This enabled me to pray that the islands would see and experience God, although I still had no idea of the plan of God to use me like He did.

2. The sensitivity to the Spirit of God also meant that the second day I was able to sense and recognise the unction of the Spirit of God to speak. Being sensitive to the Spirit of God keeps

us from being distracted even from the normal day to day events we are often surrounded with.

3. This has to do with prayer. It will be impossible to see any move of God that was not birthed in prayer. This has been a running theme through this book. The effectual fervent prayer of a righteous man avails much. Elijah had much fruit in his ministry because he prayed. He was a man of like passion like us who prayed for there to be rain and it rained. He also prayed for there to be no rain and again the heavens withheld the rains in answer to the request of this mighty man of God.

   All the past moves and revivals that we have often heard of or read of have been birthed in prayer and if we want to see significant changes in the course of history and change in the destinies of others where they are delivered from darkness into light then we must make prayer our closest ally. Prayer must become almost as natural as breathing.

4. Another key to the move that took place in the Haiti market is obedience to God and a staunch determination to respect God's prompting, commandment and leading above man's opinions or ideas. We need to realise that our walk with God is a personal one and while we might have heard from God, it does not necessarily mean that even our closest friends or leaders have heard from God on exactly the same issue. This is why we must make a steadfast decision to abide by what we have heard God say to us.

   Despite my friends not feeling the stirring of the Spirit of God like I did, it was still God that was moving me and had I walked away from the market that day and not obeyed the prompting of the Lord to speak as he wanted me to, I would have been held accountable before God.

5. The fifth key had to do with the fact that the power of God was present to heal. The atmosphere in the market became charged that day with the presence of God making it easy for salvations, healings and miracles to break through.
6. When we are motivated by love we cannot fail. It was love that made Jesus give himself on the cross for us to be saved. He would have come to die even if it was just for one person. Love motivates us to give all for Jesus and follow Him. Our love for souls will motive us to reach out to those who need Jesus the most whether it is convenient for us or not.
7. A very important key to this move in Haiti market is the faithfulness of Jesus. We can trust in Jesus totally once we have decided to obey Him in the walk of the harvest of souls that He will be faithful to bring breakthroughs that will bring a harvest. He was faithful to provide me with an interpreter and a ministry team even when this was not prepared for. A crusade was not planned, but Jesus was faithful to lead me to a big thriving Haiti market where He had already prepared masses of people to be harvested into His kingdom.

I know of no other person than the Lord Jesus who we can completely trust to bring to pass all He has said He will do. My adventure with Jesus is a daily delight and to everyone who will unashamedly immerse themselves in the river of His Spirit and daily pick up their cross to follow Him, a rich reward of His faithfulness will await you everywhere you turn. We will find that resting in His arms, the work of the kingdom is a delight rather than a tiresome chore.

Chapter Eight

God Breathes Life in The Valley of Dry Bones

So I prophesied as I was commanded. And as I was prophesying, there was a noise, a rattling sound, and the bones came together, bone to bone. I looked, and tendons and flesh appeared on them and skin covered them, but there was no breath in them.

Then he said to me, "Prophesy to the breath; prophesy, son of man, and say to it, 'This is what the Sovereign Lord says: Come, breath, from the four winds and breathe into these slain, that they may live.'" So I prophesied as he commanded me, and breath entered them; they came to life and stood up on their feet—a vast army". Ezekiel 37:7-10

I want to talk about what happens when we partner with God in these end times to bring forth those things not in existence yet which are in God's heart. What happens when we believe God absolutely even though we might find ourselves in the valley of dry bones like Ezekiel did.

Ezekiel 37 talks about the hand of the Lord bringing Ezekiel out and by the Spirit of the Lord setting him in the midst of very dry bones in a valley.

The hand of the Lord is often known to signify great power and authority, bringing deliverance especially in situations of

great difficulty. In Deuteronomy 26:8, it says the Lord brought the Israelites out of Egypt with a strong hand and a powerful arm. Isaiah 53 talks about the arm of the Lord as pertaining to salvation. Often when we walk by the Spirit of the Lord we can be an extension of His arm to bring salvation to many.

While preparing for a meeting in New York, I once had a vision of the hand of the Lord coming into the room. It was a massive and outstretched hand and I felt then the Lord was saying to me that the body of Christ needs to have an understanding of the capability of His hands to bring deliverance and provision in any situation in which we might find ourselves. So when the hand of the Lord came into Ezekiel's situation, understandably he would have been in awe and in great excitement must have wondered where the hand of the Lord was going to take him.

Ezekiel was also very much in the Spirit when the hand of the Lord came to him. When we are walking in the Spirit where the river of God is flowing, the river of God andHis Hand can often times take us where we least expect. Sometimes it might not even be where our human understanding expects us to be led to or where we might generally expect great miracles to take place. It might be a very difficult place where breakthroughs or miracles are not even known to happen.

So the Lord deposited Ezekiel where he probably least expected, in the midst of the valley of dry bones which were very dry indeed. There ensued a conversation between God and Ezekiel where God started asking Ezekiel if the bones could live. Although Ezekiel answered that God knew if the dry bones could come to life or not, God made it very clear to Ezekiel that it was up to him to prophesy in order for the dry bones to be brought to life.

According to Proverbs 18:21,

'The tongue has the power of life and death'

If Romans 4:17 describes God as a God who brings life to the dead and calls things that are not as though they are, then surely God knew what He was doing when He told Ezekiel that the answer to reviving the dead bones was to prophesy or call forth. He knows we are made in His image and if God calls things to life by the power of His words then we can do the same. Where the Spirit of the Lord is moving even in the valley of dry bones, God's words through us can release enough power to bring transformation to our cities, nations and neighbourhoods. This is a very important key in bringing in revival and a harvest of souls.

Ezekiel prophesied and there was a rattling as the dry bones came together. Flesh came upon the bones but still it was dead flesh. Ezekiel's Spirit must have keyed into what happened in Genesis 1 during creation. Although most biblical translations have Genesis 1:2 as the Spirit of the Lord *moving* upon the waters, the NRSV version of the Bible translates Genesis 1:2 *'as darkness covered the face of the deep, while a wind from God swept over the face of the waters'.* Ezekiel received the revelation that these four winds carried revival and the power to create life out of death. He understood that right there in the valley of the dry bones the winds of God were present to help release life to the words He commanded.

So Ezekiel prophesied to the four winds to call forth the breath of God and life came and entered the bodies before him until they became a vast army filled with life and power. I very much believe this vision points to the times we are living in where God can come into cities and nations to bring life and transformation when we partner with Him to decree the words of the kingdom with great power and authority.

Gothenburg, Sweden May 2010
An impartation of fire for harvest

I have been sharing about how walking by the Spirit and flowing in the river of God makes all the difference with how effective bringing in the harvest of souls can be. What occurred in Sweden in 2010 is no different.

As in Ezekiel 37, the hand of the Lord will pick up the willing believer (the one whose heart and mind is stayed on Him to see the Lord bring breakthrough for harvest) and take them into the place where they are needed the most. This might be in a place of dryness or barrenness where there has been little breakthrough in the bringing in of the harvest of souls.

Be encouraged because the Lord is always willing to pour out His Spirit in every valley of dry bones. An exceedingly great army is waiting to be brought forth from those who are dead in their trespasses and sins if we can persevere in believing the Lord and partner with Him to call forth things that are not as though they are. As in Ezekiel 37, the Lord is calling out to the believer to 'prophesy that the bones may live.'

What occurred in Sweden happened over two ministry trips so it is worth mentioning what happened during both trips. The first time I was invited to speak in Sweden was in May 2010. As with all other trips I began to ponder on the mind of God and I believed this would be a trip that God would release His Spirit to bring in the harvest. I reasoned that if the Lord had done this on previous trips, He will do the same again because Jesus Christ is the same yesterday, today and forever.

Before the trip, I had a conversation with a friend of mine and we discussed my forthcoming visit to Sweden. He told me he had lived in Sweden for several years in the past and had never

witnessed a person giving their heart to Jesus there. He said that there were many physically beautiful people there who were very reserved and that it was not easy to reach their hearts with the gospel.

How we pray matters a lot in situations where we are called to bring in the harvest in hard ground. I began to meditate on Psalms 24:9

> *"Lift up your heads, you gates; lift them up, you ancient doors, that the King of glory may come in".*

I also remembered the words of a popular Christmas song 'Let earth receive her king'. I figured that hearts and minds needed to be open to receive the ministry of Jesus in Sweden. I began to pray that the spiritual gates of the cities in Sweden would open to the ministry of Jesus. I decreed that the King of glory, Jesus, would come in unhindered. The Lord led me in prayer to speak to the land in Sweden and to the hearts of the Swedish people, to open and receive the ministry of Jesus.

It was in the process of praying that one night before my first trip to Sweden, the Lord gave me a dream.

In the dream, I was walking towards a place and about to cross a bridge in order to get there. Before I could cross the bridge, a powerful being appeared beside me and held my left hand. As he held my left hand in his, I felt in my spirit that he was releasing an impartation into my hand which was needed for the journey ahead of me. I woke up and knew what I had received was for my ministry in Sweden.

The ministry started with a school of Prophetic Evangelism where I taught from John 4 the story of Jesus with the Samaritan woman at the well. I shared that Jesus was confident of the wells

of living water that He had inside Him. He knew this was what the woman needed but He could also discern that this precious Samaritan woman had lots of walls which had been built up in her heart as a result of the long standing hostility between the Jews and Samaritans. Jesus knew He had to get beyond these walls and gain her trust in order for her to receive willingly what He had for her.

Jesus asked her to give him water and she immediately uttered out loud her surprise at a Jew asking her for water. Jesus told her that if only she knew Who was asking her for water she would be asking Him for the living waters He had so that she would never thirst again. She wondered at being able to have waters that would quench her thirst forever. Greatly desiring to have this water, she asked Jesus to give her the water.

Jesus fully knowing she had no husband asked her to go and bring her husband. After the Samaritan woman replied that she didn't have a husband, Jesus told her she had previously had five husbands and the man she was now living with was not her husband. His accuracy amazed her and she immediately believed in Him. She then went about telling everyone she had met the Messiah who had told her everything about herself.

Many times when the Lord gives us prophetic words for the unsaved, we need to try as much as possible to come to a level of understanding about the heart of the unsaved, so that we can gain their trust. Jesus did not just go to the woman and say 'I have wells of living waters and I know you have had five husbands'. That would have been true but it might have alienated her from receiving the truth. He had to gently break through her walls before revealing these truths to her.

First of all, He gained her trust by asking her the right questions. By gaining her trust, He brought her from the point where she was distrustful of Him simply because He was a Jew to where she became curious of the wells of living waters He had. She then desired the living waters that would quench her thirst forever because she really was a seeker just like most people on the earth today.

Most people are seeking redemption although many are looking in the wrong places. She then became a believer when Jesus told her she had had five husbands and demonstrated to her He was the Messiah who knew all things.

Like Jesus, when we are fully aware of who we are and what we have in Christ, then we are confident to know what the world needs. When we give prophetic words to the unsaved, it is not to demonstrate that we accurately hear God, but it is to draw the unsaved to the Father by sharing the message of the gospel. Jesus, as the redeemer of the world, did not only give the woman an accurate prophetic word, He also made her understand that if she drunk His living waters she would be redeemed from eternal thirst. Her redemption would come when she believed in Him as the Messiah.

I mentioned the above because I have heard several believers who were so content to have been able to release an accurate prophetic word to the unsaved, that in the excitement of the moment they just simply walked away without ever sharing the gospel. When the heart of the unsaved is open after receiving such an encouraging prophetic word, it is the best time to share the gospel of Jesus with them. The Holy Spirit does the conviction of sin, while we simply need to be obedient to the commandment of Jesus to preach the gospel.

After the session on prophetic evangelism, I called for those who would like to receive an impartation of fire and boldness from the Lord for the work of the harvest in Sweden. I knew in the dream I had before coming to Sweden I had received an impartation of fire which was critical for what was going to take place. Several people came forward and the Lord released His fiery impartation of boldness on them.

In Acts 2, we have the baptism of the Holy Spirit and fire that took place preceding the revival which ensued from the infilling of the Holy Spirit. The disciples of Jesus became bold after they were baptized with the Holy Spirit and with fire and they began to preach the gospel with great boldness and power. I believe this to be an important precedent for us to follow today. We are to hunger for and receive the fire for the harvest the same way the disciples did.

After sharing at this school of evangelism in Sweden, I then prayed a prayer of impartation of the release of the Spirit's fire over the believers. At the end of the meeting, we decided to go to one of the malls in Gothenburg to minister the love of Jesus. The mall was very busy when we arrived with an array of different nationalities and we met with Muslims of different nationalities.

The atmosphere was open as many of the team began to share the gospel. The people seemed friendly and open as we ministered in a relaxed atmosphere. Many were happy to talk to the team and to hear about the gospel of Jesus.

As I ministered with the team, we approached an older Swedish lady who shared how lonely she had been feeling. We shared the love of Jesus with her and she wept unashamedly as we led her to the Lord. What a glorious day of salvation that proved to be for her.

Another lady felt the presence of God all over her as I led her to the Lord with the team. She asked us why she felt goose bumps all over as I prayed for her. We explained that it was the presence of the Lord showing He was near her and allowing her to feel His presence. The Lord was doing marvelously as He continued moving in the lives of people with His convicting presence.

After some time, I felt I had to go and rest and prepare for the evening service but as I turned to go, I felt the Lord tell me to look behind me. I turned back and saw a tall and beautiful Swedish lady, probably in her twenties, walking into the mall. She looked like one of these beautiful Swedish people that my friend had told me about who were extremely reserved but I felt the Lord was leading me to go and speak to her.

I approached her with a wide smile and I told her I was visiting from London. As we started to chat, she told me how happy she was that I came to talk to her as people hardly spoke to her in Sweden and as a result she was very lonely. My heart went out to her as I wondered how such a confident and beautiful looking lady could have been so lonely. You just could not tell from her facade but the Lord knew what was behind those walls in her heart just like He knew the Samaritan woman so well. This was a lady that was seeking love and acceptance just like so many people are.

I told her I was a Christian and shared my story with her about how the Lord saved me from depression and the brink of suicide. She looked at me and said she had been thinking of committing suicide too. My heart was filled with compassion as I shared how much the Lord loved her. I told her He loved her unconditionally and He would accept her just the way she was. I asked her if she would like to receive the Lord who loved her so unconditionally into her heart and she said yes.

My heart overflowed with joy as I led her in a prayer of repentance and salvation. After she had received Jesus Christ into her heart, I asked her how she felt and she said she felt beautiful. Her face was glowing and I wondered at the love of Jesus and the eyes of the Lord that saw this woman and caught my attention so I did not pass her by. He will often ask us to stop for just the one because His heart burns for the lost whether they are one or a multitude.

The Pastor of the church named Pastor Isaacs who invited me to speak in Sweden told me how encouraged he was with what the Lord did. He told me he and his wife had tried to do street evangelism in Sweden years ago but no one ever responded. He told me they became disappointed and had stopped doing outreaches for a while. He was encouraged when he saw how the Lord opened the heart of the people we met as they spoke to their church team. He was amazed at the openness in the atmosphere and the goodness of God in saving those who came to Him. He made a decision to continue reaching out to the lost again in Sweden.

What an amazing God we have. When there is an outpouring of the Spirit of God, the work of the harvest becomes so much easier. The impartation of the fire of the Lord on God's people also emboldens them.

As I have done throughout this book, I will endeavour to share why the work of the harvest in the first part of the ministry to Sweden was successful so that you can lay hold of important keys in this move of the harvesting of souls. It is my heart's desire that breakthroughs will be experienced by all willing to partake of this work of the end time harvest.

Firstly, I believe the prayers that were prayed for the Swedish trip were very pivotal to how God moved on the trip. I knew

that for the ministry in Sweden to be successful, hearts must be opened and softened to receive the word of the Lord. I discerned that the spiritual atmosphere in Sweden must be open to receive the ministry of Jesus, so I prayed Psalm 24 commanding and decreeing that the spiritual gates and ancient doors in Sweden would open to receive the ministry of Jesus. I prayed that the gates in the hearts of people that had been shut would be open to receive Jesus.

Often, praying specific prayers when we have received a revelation from the Lord on how to pray will quickly open doors that had previously been shut. I believe it was this type of prayer that caused hearts to be so open to our ministry. The Lord himself is the door opener and by praying these prayers, it allowed him to answer the prayers by opening hearts that had been locked against him.

One of the most powerful ways of gaining entrance into hearts so that they can receive the gospel of Jesus is through prayers.

Secondly, the visitation I had in the dream where I was imparted with the fire of the Lord was also very significant for the breakthrough in Gothenburg. This fiery impartation was carried into the meeting and as God's people received impartation and were baptized into this fire of holy boldness, they were able to minister in the power and love of Jesus in the mall. The heart cry of the Lord is for us to be endued with his power and fire. I believe if we will tarry with the Lord and receive his fire like the disciples we will experience great breakthrough in bringing a multitude of harvest to the kingdom.

Next, I believe the wisdom with which the Lord led me to share about how He ministered to the woman by the well was also an important key that led to the people we encountered to be open

to the gospel as we ministered. We approached the people we met at the mall in a relaxed and friendly manner which also helped to break down their walls.

We were confident like Jesus that we had the wells of living waters that they needed, yet we took time out to get to know those we met, to find out about them and hear their heart before we released the word of the Lord we had for them.

In summary, a combination of Spirit-led specific prayers, the impartation of the fire of the Lord and the attitude of love, boldness and friendliness with which we approached those in Sweden, led to hearts being open to receive the gospel of Jesus.

March 2011 – Gothenburg

The events that took place in May 2010 in Gothenburg had stirred up such increased hunger for the harvest that another opportunity opened up to minister from the same church that had invited me before, this time in evangelistic events across Sweden in Angered Centrum and other venues in Gothenburg.

I heard the good news that Pastor Isaacs of 'I am that I am' ministries church in Gothenburg, who I had worked with the previous year, had actively started street outreach again with his church team. This was good news indeed to hear that within that year their church had been reaching out with the good news of Jesus again.

We started with a revival meeting at Agape church in Gothenburg. I shared on the river of God and what happens when the tide of the river of God rises. When this happens, we see an increase in supernatural healings, signs and wonders and increase of salvations. Many were touched by God's fiery presence and the hunger that had been fanned by Jesus just kept increasing and

there was increased expectation for what the Lord was about to do.

The next couple of days were spent teaching on a healing and evangelistic school hosted by 'I am that I am' ministries. This was a training school on prophetic evangelism and healing activation. I love the fact that they were so eager to hear the heart of God for the lost.

> *"You have multiplied, O LORD my God, your wondrous deeds and your thoughts toward us; none can compare with you! Were I to proclaim and tell of them, they would be more than can be counted.".* Psalm 40:5 NRSV

If we as believers can connect to just one thought that God has for an unsaved person, I believe they will be amazed at the loving kindness of God. His heart constantly burns for the lost and His thoughts for them are to restore them to Him in His loving kindness. If we are able to connect to one individual word for the unsaved and communicate it to them, the unsaved can be encouraged to believe in a loving God who loves and thinks constantly about them.

It is not unusual to see the unsaved break down in tears when confronted with such a loving word from God. I believe the prophetic was activated that night as several opened up their heart in their godly desire to hear His voice regarding those He loves so much.

I believe very much in supernatural healing and believe that God is calling the body of Christ to preach the gospel with demonstrations of His power, signs and wonders. I shared with the class God's desire for His people to fulfil the mandate of healing the sick. The early disciples were our forerunners and examples as they went about preaching the gospel. Sometimes

thousands became believers of Jesus. Many were healed and several were delivered of demonic presence. This was the ministry of Jesus who went about doing good and healing all those who were oppressed by the devil. We are called, mandated and given authority to do the same.

I believed the Lord wanted to release a healing activation in the class in Sweden, but I also felt He wanted to impart boldness and confidence within the believers so that they could actively heal the sick as they had been called to.

I began to feel the healing fire burning in parts of my body. Usually the way I know that God is going to heal someone or when someone is being healed in a meeting is by feeling the manifest burning presence of the Lord in that area of my body. I knew God wanted to heal in this meeting. I could sense that several were sick and had infirmities in their bodies and where there is sickness or infirmity, I know it is the desire of the Lord to heal.

However, I could also discern it was also for impartation for healing in the believers. One of the works of the five-fold ministry is to edify and build the body so we all come into manifest fullness in Christ. So I knew the Lord wanted and desired to bring fullness in the work of healing in the church.

I prayed over the students that God would release His healing impartation over them and activate them to do works of healing. I then called out words of knowledge for different sicknesses and conditions. As those affected with sicknesses stood up, I felt led by God to ask some of the students who had been activated into healing to lay hands and pray for those who were sick. They were to command and decree that sicknesses would leave the bodies of those who were sick.

The students prayed for the sick and I asked those who were prayed for to test their bodies to see if they had been healed. It was hilariously joyful to see the surprise on both of those who were prayed for and those who prayed. Those who were prayed for, were joyful they were healed and felt no more pain, while those who prayed for the sick looked at each other as if to say 'Did I just do that?'

This demonstrated that the Lord is no respecter of persons. He longs to and will use anyone who is willing to heal the sick and save the lost at this hour. He just needs willing hearts for heaven to visit and impart His people with the fullness of destiny. Thank you Jesus for continually activating the saints to do the work of revival!

I also gave a word at the meeting that God wanted them to breathe in the Holy Ghost. I made a call for those who had not spoken in tongues and several came forward and a teenage girl began to speak in tongues. I decided to ask the others how they felt. One of them said she felt so empty. Filled with compassion, I asked the teenage girl who had begun to speak in tongues to lay hands on her while I prayed. Soon she was slain in the Spirit and she began to speak in tongues.

Clearly, it could be seen that the Lord was actively increasing the working of the Holy Spirit so that the precious saints in Sweden could see supernatural healings, signs and wonders in addition to the outreach ministries they were beginning to do again.

It was interesting to see so many nationalities in Gothenburg as we encountered different nationalities as we ministered in a well-known mall called Angered Centrum. We experienced more of the openness we had seen the Lord release during my last visit. Several were open to chat with us and what a delight it

was to see people give their hearts to Jesus. During some of the outreaches, we also prayed for the sick too.

Boras, March 25, 2011

The meetings in Sweden had been gaining momentum in the outpouring of the Spirit. The Lord was pouring out His Spirit as He promised He would do in the last days. This was a fulfilment of the word of the Lord when He said in Acts 2:17 that He would pour out of His Spirit upon all flesh. The unsaved and the infirm were receiving the benefits of the outpouring of the Spirit of the Lord on their lives and many were greatly encouraged at what the Lord was doing.

Earlier on in the chapter when I wrote about Ezekiel 37, it was the events that took place in Boras, Sweden, that made me share on this chapter.

Barrenness, sickness, iniquity and sin always necessitate the hand of the Lord to move and intervene on behalf of those affected.

Isaiah 53 describes the arm of the Lord in the person of Jesus as He bore our sins and transgressions and took away our sicknesses. Jesus had to do this under great pain and torment as He was whipped, broken, bruised and nailed to the cross suffering the greatest pain for mankind so He could destroy the works of the devil and redeem mankind from the slavery and bondage of sin and sickness.

1 John 4:17 says we are as Jesus is on the earth. If Jesus who is the author and finisher of our faith was the arm of the Lord revealed to take away sin, sickness and suffering from this world, then we are surely called to be like Him on this earth. God sees where we do not often see and the cries of the unsaved

continually go to Him. When we have no knowledge of where there is an urgent need for His saving arm and grace, He will intervene by stretching forth His hand to bring us into a place where we are needed the most.

Such is the walk of the Spirit and being led by the Spirit. At a moment's notice, the Lord can change the course of our direction and bring us to a place where we are needed the most in order to set people free so that Jesus can be glorified.

I felt that certainly the hand of the Lord was instrumental in picking me up and bringing me into what I could only describe as the valley of dry bones in Boras, Sweden.

By this time, I had been ministering in several places in Sweden holding revival meetings, training schools and leading outreaches, so understandably my physical body had become somewhat tired. This was how I felt on the night when the host pastor from Gothenburg came to take me to an all-night prayer meeting in Boras. He told me I had been invited to speak and minister at this meeting.

This type of all-night prayer meeting would often have prayers and worship offered up until the following morning. I was told that Boras would be significantly colder than Gothenburg and that it was also a very long drive.

As my mind began to process all this information, I began to think as a human being is prone to do even when we should really be led by the Spirit at all times! I thought of how much I hated the cold and how I had not brought many warm clothes for the trip. I thought of how tired I felt and how badly I needed to rest that night. I felt that my physical body just was not ready to minister at an all-night prayer meeting! Perhaps I felt the priority was for me to rest and be prepared for the rest of the meetings and outreaches I was meant to minister at on the rest of the trip.

God had not told me that revival was going to break out at the all-night prayer meeting, so I was not even thinking of the possibility. As I pondered in my mind whether to refuse the invitation, the host pastor took a look at my face and perhaps reading some of the thoughts fleeting through my expressive face, he said maybe I should rest if I was that tired as there were still other meetings that we were going to be doing for the rest of the time in Sweden. But even as he gave me that way out, I began to feel a sense of unease that it was not God's best and I told him I would go to Boras.

We began the long journey to Boras and found the venue. It was much colder than Gothenburg so I was looking forward to entering into the venue where I could be warm. To my surprise it was at an uncompleted building in a park with no windows or doors. I learned that it was the first time the host had scheduled the meeting in the venue. Previous meetings had been held in completed buildings. He had also had to request for a permit from the police to hold the meeting, which could be described as an open air meeting in a public place!

We entered the building and as we did so, I felt the chilly wind blow in. I am usually not very comfortable with very cold areas and with open spaces and no doors or windows in place, I felt very uncomfortable indeed. In my heart I had not yet connected to the intent and purpose of God for the meeting, all my flesh could feel was the intense cold and the chilly wind.

I began to complain in my mind thinking to myself 'This place is so cold, how can I cope staying here all night till the morning. God, surely you know how much I hate the cold. I love to obey you but this is so hard. I have been ministering and I am tired and now I am likely to catch a cold. Why have a meeting in an uncompleted building, I do not understand this.

As I was complaining, I did not know what I expected but I suspect I was expecting God to give me a pat on the head or something but the Lord did not mince words with me. He spoke to me and told me quite sternly to quit complaining so that I would not hinder what He was about to do that night. There was a hush moment in my soul and I felt the fear of the Lord as I knew for the first time the Lord had a hand in bringing me to that place.

Like Ezekiel, I had been brought by the hand of the Lord into *"a valley of dry bones."* He had not brought me into a beautiful place where my flesh would be comfortable but into a dry and desolate place where his Spirit was longing to move. I repented and asked the Lord to forgive me and I made a decision to come in agreement with whatever He had planned to do that night.

I understood afresh what the Lord meant when we are asked to die daily. Dying one day is not enough but we are called into a daily walk with Jesus to crucify our flesh and walk in the Spirit taking our cross daily. My flesh was uncomfortable with the intense cold and because I had not discerned God's plan to bring revival into that area, it was initially hard for me to want to stay where the Lord had need of me.

But thank God even when we are not immediately aware that we are in the midst of the will of the Lord, if we listen for His voice, He will speak to us and align us to bring about His will for our lives.

Some reading this book might be in physical place of extreme dryness and you might not even have recognized why you are where you are. I will encourage you to still your heart and listen for His will because it might be the Lord who has brought you by His mighty and outstretched hand into the place where you are to demonstrate His glory. If you partner with the Lord, He longs to fill the valley you are in, with pools of His glory and revival fire so that all will experience His goodness.

I joined in the praise and worship as the believers began to raise their voice in vibrant and wholehearted praise to Jesus. As I worshipped and praised, my attention suddenly focused on two Swedish ladies that I saw standing outside who were laughing, giggling and staring at us. I left the building and walked outside to talk with them.

I introduced myself to them and said I was visiting from the United Kingdom and asked them where they were coming from. They told me they were coming from a party being held in a pub or bar somewhere around the place where we were gathering to worship and pray. They asked what we were doing and I explained to them that we were praising God and singing songs to Him because we were happy to be Christians and we were happy to praise our God who was so exciting and alive.

They looked at me and asked in surprise 'You guys are a church?' And they commented that all the churches they had known in Sweden seemed so boring in comparison. They seemed to be happy with what they saw: 'A vibrant gathering of happy believers not ashamed to worship their God openly.'

I shared the gospel with them about God who sent His Son Jesus Christ to die for the sins of the world because He loves us and wants to have a relationship with us. They listened and just kept on smiling. I sensed they were open to the gospel and seizing the opportunity, I asked them if they would like to receive Jesus into their hearts. They said yes, so I explained that if they would pray and ask for forgiveness of sins from God, Jesus would come into their hearts and save them.

They prayed with me and invited Jesus into their hearts as Saviour. It was such a joyous moment and they even gave me their phone number so I could give their number to the leader

of the group. They were interested in connecting and becoming part of the Christian community.

As the worship and praise progressed in the meeting, my eyes were drawn to more and more people coming near where we were worshipping. When I questioned them, they told me they were coming from pubs, bars and parties in the area. It turned out that we were having the meeting in the part of Boras that never seems to sleep. It was the centre of nightlife where people regularly frequented to have a nice night out and have fun.

I began to discern that the prophet who organized the all-night prayer meeting in that area had acted with great discernment. It was truly under the direction of God and by holding the meeting in an uncompleted building without doors or windows, it meant that we were able to see and be in contact with the many people who were passing near that area during the night.

It seemed to me that this is a picture of the body of Christ the Lord wants us to be like. A church without barriers and without walls where we can easily see and be seen by those who would like to reach out to and be saved and delivered by Jesus who we carry within us. The lack of windows and doors in the building was a slight inconvenience compared to the need that was around us.

In Ezekiel 37:2, Ezekiel was led back and forth between the dry bones. There was no doubt that he was meant to focus on the dry bones so he could gain understanding that he had been brought into the valley because there was a need. As the meeting went on, the Lord kept capturing my eyes back and forth amongst those who were walking past. These were the dry bones that needed to experience the life of God so that the breath could come into them so that they could become living beings in their Spirit as they came to know Jesus as Lord and Saviour.

Several of those I talked with outside were giving their lives to Jesus. The atmosphere was so open. It began to be evident that a fresh wind of the Spirit of the Lord was blowing in the area. By this time I noticed I was no longer feeling cold. The move of the Spirit was such that all I could do was focus on was what the Lord was doing. By this time also, the prophet leading the prayer meeting had begun to hear about those who were getting saved in the area. He gave glory to God at the reports and after a while invited me to come and speak the words the Lord had given me for the meeting.

I had not prepared a message to speak before-hand but as I took the microphone, I felt a fresh wind blow in. It was different from the cold and chilly winds which I had naturally felt. This was a wind of revival that was blowing in the place. In Ezekiel 37, life had blown in and entered into the slain in the valley of dry bones because Ezekiel had called forth the breath of God from the four winds so that they could enter into the slain bodies.

Where darkness, iniquity and sin abounds, we can be rest assured that the presence of the Holy Spirit or the winds of God will not be far from that area, because this is what is needed to bring life and resurrection into the places where Jesus is needed the most.

If we choose to speak life at all times, then His presence around us will bring forth His words in us. I continued to share in the meeting about the hand of God that was strongly present in that place to bring about His will and purpose. I shared that the wind of the Lord had blown into the place so as to give life to the dry bones so they could bring forth flesh and become an exceeding great and mighty army.

As I shared, I felt the Lord begin to speak to me that while we had planned to have an all-night prayer meeting, He had intervened and it had, instead, become an evangelistic crusade. This was indeed a Spirit-led evangelism orchestrated and designed by the Lord of Hosts, Himself.

I shared about the many who the Lord was longing to touch and breathe into that night. I felt that those who were dead in their trespasses and sins, the Lord wanted to quicken by His Spirit according to Ephesians 2:1.

As I shared, I looked behind me and I saw some Swedish men who had gathered watching and listening from a distance as if transfixed. There was no worship or music to attract anyone and yet the presence of the Lord drew them there. I looked at them and addressed them. I declared to them that the meeting was for them and that the Lord wanted their hearts because He loves them. Because He loved them, He came to die for them and if they would believe and receive Him into their hearts asking for the forgiveness of sins, they would be forgiven and He would be their Saviour.

I gave them an invitation, asking if they would like to receive Jesus as their Lord and Saviour and they said yes. If it had not been for the presence of the Lord drawing them to Him, I doubt anything could have made them leave where they had been and walk all the way into the building where we were having the meeting! They stood in the building and prayed joyfully asking Jesus to come into their hearts and save them.

What an amazing work of the Holy Spirit to convict hearts indeed! We need never be afraid of ever speaking His words of love and power to those who needs Him. We only need to obey and He, the Holy Spirit, will bring the conviction upon hearts.

In John 16:8, Jesus said the Holy Spirit will convict the world concerning sin, righteousness and judgment. We can trust the Holy Spirit to do the work He does best.

As the meeting progressed, more and more people who were coming from partying came into the building, drawn by the loving presence of the Lord. They gladly and joyfully received Jesus into their hearts.

It was a glorious night to remember. The hearts of the believers were encouraged and those who received Jesus did so gladly as they encountered the Saviour in the way that was not expected by them. The Lord sent His wind to blow in the spiritually dead valley of dry bones in Boras and quickened the souls of men with his Spirit, so they could experience newness of life. We must always give God all the glory when we experience such a revival or a move of God.

There was an overflow from this meeting on Friday night in Boras to the following Saturday when we had another outreach in Gothenburg. This was an open-air outreach where the host pastor opened the meeting by preaching in the power of the Holy Ghost. I spoke afterwards and shared my testimony on how I came to know Jesus. As I finished speaking I remember a Muslim woman running from a long way off to come and listen to the preaching which had finished before she could get there. She decided to come to the church meeting the following Sunday.

Such was the hunger for the presence of the Lord which was felt tangibly by those we came in contact with during these events in Sweden that Romans 8:19 was brought to life:

> *"For the creation waits in eager expectation for the children of God to be revealed."*

There is a travailing and groaning going on all over the earth from God's creation, who in their spirits desire salvation and a deliverance from every bondage and curse. When we live a life that seeks to manifest Christ and His presence in every way, then we can increasingly become answers to people's needs and their needs for salvation. For as Christ is, so are we called to be on this earth.

In summary, I will share why I believe the move of God took place, particularly in Boras. The aim as always is to show and demonstrate everywhere that God is able and willing to release revival in any place, town, city or country regardless of the situation if we will partner with Him in faith.

Firstly, I believe the choices we make play an integral part in how much of the move of God we experience in our lives. At the point where the host pastor in Gothenburg came to pick me up to go and minister in Boras, I was physically tired and tempted just to rest. I had not heard from God regarding what He wanted to do. I could have stayed when I got the green light from the host pastor and taken time out to rest for the other meetings, but the nagging feeling of unease in me made me decide to press in and go to Boras.

Let us not neglect to be led by God in every way even if it is through the still small voice or a check in our spirit. The most powerful moves I have experienced have always been when I have yielded to or walked by the Spirit of God.

Secondly, we must guard our hearts with all diligence for from our hearts spring the wellsprings of life. God had to address my heart and my thoughts when I was at the meeting in Boras. Some might think that complaining is a normal reaction due to the discomfort of worshipping in a building without doors or

windows which made exposure to the cold winds even more difficult. But the Lord rightly told me to stop complaining because if I had remained in that attitude, my heart could have shut out the springs of living waters from flowing out of me.

God's ways are not our ways! The prophet who was leading the meeting was led by God to hold it in that part of Boras. Without windows or doors we were able to see those who passed by. I would never have been able to see those outside who desperately needed Jesus if we were behind closed doors. God's plan is to have a church without walls or barriers where we can see and be seen by those who need Him the most and so we can minister His love, salvation and deliverance to them.

Next, I believe the discernment to sense what God was doing at that moment in time and His greater purpose outside the meeting was also key.

I could have decided to just completely focus on the worship taking place inside the building to the exclusion of what Jesus was drawing my attention to outside of the building. In John 4:35, Jesus had to address His disciples to look and pay attention to the fields that were ripe for harvest. Today, I believe the Lord of the harvest is doing the same. He is calling our attention to look and behold the ripeness of the harvest and become active labourers and to lose our passivity in bringing in the harvest of souls into the kingdom.

I believe that the worship and praise that was taking place inside the building was also fuelling the release of the Spirit of God that was drawing souls to come near the building from the bars and parties they were coming from.

Fourthly, I believe the wind of revival that was blowing around the area of Boras had the life needed to quicken to life those

who were dead in their trespasses and sins. The valley of dry bones came to life because of the same breath of God and the presence of God that the Lord released in Boras. Our prayers and the prophetic decrees also activated the breath of God.

Fifthly, the Holy Spirit was present. As the Lord gave me the words to speak both to the individual passers-by and to those who were watching as I preached, the Holy Spirit whose work is to draw all to Jesus began to convict the hearts the of the unsaved. Feeling the heavy convicting presence of the Holy Spirit, it was difficult for those who heard the words spoken to resist the Spirit's prompting resulting in several coming to Jesus that night.

I believe today every worker of the harvest must pray for the convicting presence of the Holy Spirit to be present as they speak. They must pray for hearts to open and receive the words lovingly spoken by the unction of the Spirit of God and that the grace of God which is appearing to all men will be received and not rejected.

Lastly is the faithfulness of God himself. The Lord is faithful and always willing to save and draw all to Himself. He loved the world so much that He gave His one and only begotten Son that whosoever would believe in Him would not perish but have everlasting life. As we partner with Him in obedience to a life of walking in the Spirit, He will be faithful to bring in the harvest that we are seeking and believing for.

The role of Jesus as the breaker who goes ahead of us to release breakthrough was also very vital in Boras. Micah 2:13 says:

> *"The One who breaks open the way will go up before them; they will break through the gate and go out'. Their king will pass through before them, the LORD at their head."*

Jesus broke open the way in every ministry that took place in Sweden to release breakthrough for harvest.

Chapter Nine

The Urgency of Our Times and Keys to Releasing the Harvest

I believe we are very much on the threshold of the end times that Jesus spoke about. There is therefore an acceleration of what is on God's heart at this time. Destinies are being launched into the purpose of God. Mantles are being released for the work of the end time harvests and there is an increase in angelic activity for the completion of the work of the end time harvest. Because of the urgency of the times we live in, heavenly assistance is being sent to those who are ready and willing to run with their destiny.

Let us take a look at the scriptures below to see what Jesus said about the signs of the end.

Here are the words of Jesus below taken from the Scripture 'Matthew 24: 3-14

> *"As Jesus was sitting on the Mount of Olives, the disciples came to him privately. "Tell us," they said, "when will this happen, and what will be the sign of your coming and of the end of the age?" Jesus answered: "Watch out that no one deceives you. For many will come in my name, claiming, 'I am the Messiah,' and will deceive many. You will hear of wars and rumours of wars, but see to it that you are not alarmed. Such things must happen, but the end is still to come. Nation will rise against nation, and kingdom against kingdom. There will be famines and earthquakes in various places. All these are the beginning*

of birth pains. Then you will be handed over to be persecuted and put to death, and you will be hated by all nations because of me. At that time many will turn away from the faith and will betray and hate each other, and many false prophets will appear and deceive many people. Because of the increase of wickedness, the love of most will grow cold, but the one who stands firm to the end will be saved. And this gospel of the kingdom will be preached in the whole world as a testimony to all nations, and then the end will come".

It is a reality that very many of these signs are already taking place. The enemy understands this and is accelerating wickedness on the earth and deception is increasing among the saints of God to cause a blindness regarding the urgency of the times we are in. The unsaved are being deceived more and more into the paths of eternal damnation but let us be assured that as darkness increases on the earth so will the light of heaven increase even more on those who are ready to arise with their heavenly armour of light.

As seen from this scripture, the world is experiencing the birth pangs of the end times, with wars and rumours of wars, earthquakes and brotherly betrayals. With an increase in deception going on within the body of Christ and amongst the unsaved, I believe we are certainly at the threshold of the end times if not in the end times itself.

It is interesting that Jesus shows us how to respond to these times. Although the love of many will grow cold, He tells us the one who stands firm till the end will be saved. He tells us the gospel of the kingdom will be preached in the whole world and then the end will come.

In other words our response to living in these times of increasing

wickedness is to stand firm in our love and faith and preach the gospel in the entire world to precede the coming of Christ. While the enemy is very much aware of the times and he reacts by increasing wickedness on the earth, we as Christians must wake up from our slumber and advance the kingdom and the gospel to all the nations as Jesus encourages and exhorts us to do.

While we might not all feel a call to travel the nations like myself or others do, cumulatively we play our part in the preaching of the gospel to all the nations by ministering His love to those who come across our paths on a daily basis. It might be on the way to do the shopping, or just relaxing in the park, but the message of the hour as I believe the Lord is saying is 'All hands on deck' Everyone must put their hands to the plough and be involved at this hour.

Throughout this book I have been talking about what happens when we are carried in the river of God. The river's powerful currents will deposit the abandoned and sold-out believers in places where they are needed the most, to bring in the harvest for Jesus and to heal wounded and broken lives. The river of God also flows with the frequency of heaven.

Because of the urgency of our times, the river of God is moving with the urgent rhythm and frequency of heaven and is depositing believers with accelerated pace to places they are need the most. The urgency is such that the matter of a person's salvation is a matter of life and death and is a choice between heaven and hell.

The story or testimony I'm writing below shows very powerfully how urgently the Spirit's flow is needed in our lives. It is also a somewhat emotional story for me but I feel that this message needs to be told to impact lives.

Before I went into full time ministry, I was working for a financial services company in the heart of London, England. I was employed as an account manager and given the responsibilities to sell our data products and services to banks and financial services companies in different countries around the world.

One of the countries I started to call was Denmark. I was calling several banks in Denmark to promote and sell my company's products, when I came in contact with a banking professional in Denmark called Eigil. He was not only willing to look into the possibility of buying our solutions but wanted to help me by contacting many of his banking colleagues to have a trial and buy the products we have to offer. He put so much effort into contacting several banks in Denmark and subsequently helping to increase my sales by building up my customer base that I was impressed by his kindness and willingness to help someone unknown to him.

As we continued to talk, he revealed to me that he was coming to visit London shortly. I began to feel an urgency in my Spirit regarding his coming, which translated into prayers. I began to pray for his salvation and that the Lord would open his heart to receive the gospel. Because I knew he was a finance professional who also happened to be the company's customer, I began to pray for wisdom on how to share the gospel with him in such a professional environment. I knew I had to be professional all through and at the same time I felt he needed to hear the gospel as soon as possible.

I approached my manager at the time and told him that the man who had been instrumental for a lot of the sales I had made for the company was coming to London and that I thought it was a good idea for the company to thank him as a company by taking him out and treating him to a meal at a nice restaurant.

The company agreed to sponsor the meal from the hospitality budget so I knew somehow God was setting a plan in motion for an environment where His heart would be revealed to this man.

I was to meet him on a Sunday and so before meeting him, I got together with the cell group I was leading in my local church. I told them about the background behind meeting him and what he did. I sensed that because he was one of the prominent people in the financial banking circles, he would be one that would have a mind set to reason things intelligently.

We all agreed that we needed to pray for God to remove every veil the god of this world had used to blind his mind and will. We prayed that he would not reason the truth of the gospel in his mind in such a way as to create a barrier but that his spirit would be touched by the Spirit of God to receive the true gospel of Jesus. We spent a while interceding for him in the Spirit and we did not stop until we felt a release in our Spirit that our prayers had been heard.

Some of you reading this book might be working in a professional work environment with various rules that have to be adhered to within a work environment. Even where there are rules forbidding sharing the gospel, you can still build friendships that will allow you to share the gospel and the love of Jesus during times of socializing such as lunch breaks or after work.

I believe Jesus will provide an opportunity or a way for the one who seeks to bring souls to Him either on the mission field or in the market place. I have heard believers give reasons as to why they could not share the gospel with their work colleagues but from my experience, showing great professionalism and excelling at work when I was in the marketplace gave me plenty of opportunities to share the reason for the hope of my call. For

example, I remember that when I was asked by managers and work colleagues why I often excelled at work, I simply told them it was due to the favour of God, which was a cause of interest for them. They became so interested that this allowed me to share the gospel with some of them.

It was indeed the favour of God that had opened a door for the Danish finance professional to help bring business to me and he worked so hard to do this also and this opened the door for his salvation too.

During the Sunday he was arriving, we agreed to meet at Notting Hill Gate close to the Kensington Temple church I was attending that night. I took him to a nice Italian restaurant close by. As we sat down to a nice meal, we began to discuss various subjects regarding work and business. As we talked, in my Spirit I kept on praying for the right words to say to open up a conversation about the gospel of Jesus in a way that would not seem awkward with the conversation we were having. We can be full of the Spirit and the power of God but we still need wisdom and sensitivity on occasions in relating with people in similar special circumstances which I was in.

As we talked, I noticed how happy he looked and my mind wondered to an article I had read beforehand describing the Danish people as the happiest people on earth. Suddenly I knew this was my cue to open up the conversation about Jesus I so desperately needed to have with him.

I looked at him and said "Eigil, I have read that the Danish people are the happiest people on earth, why do you think that is?' He answered me and said it was for various reasons. He said in his case it was because of his family and other various things he mentioned. I told him I was very happy too for these reasons

but even more so because of my personal faith in Jesus. Jesus had given me the common ground I needed to be able to share the gospel with him.

In the training schools on evangelism I hold in different churches, one of the practical ways I teach on successfully reaching out to people is trying to find a common ground with them in conversation that will serve as a launching pad to sharing the gospel or a prophetic word given us by the Lord to them.

I often joke that when reaching out to the English in Britain I find the common ground by talking about the weather. It never fails as a talking point. If the weather was rainy they would go on about how much they hate a rainy day and if it was hot they would be so excited about how much they love a sunny day. This openness then gives me the opportunity to develop a conversation with them from there which leads to a message about the gospel.

In Eigil's case, my common ground was found when I talked about how I have heard that the Danish were the happiest on earth. I built on that common ground by boldly and lovingly telling him that while I had things like family that made me happy, there was a vacuum inside of me which could never have been filled up if I never believed in Jesus. I told him that he and everyone had that same vacuum too and nothing else could fill it except Jesus. I shared my testimony with him about how depressed and suicidal I was while growing up and how Jesus coming into my heart, filled the empty hole I had in me, healed my depression and saved me.

As if it was yesterday, I still remember looking at him across the dinner table and the new light that shone in his eyes as he gained understanding of what I was saying. I asked him if he would like to receive Jesus as Lord and Saviour in his heart and to my delight

this amazing man said yes. I led him to say a prayer of salvation and right there in the restaurant a new man was born in Christ.

It was time to go to my local evening church service by the time we finished dinner and I asked him if he would like to go to church with me. With his new found faith in him, he was happy to go with me to church. While at church before the service started, I took him to the church bookshop and bought him a book by Roberts Lairdon in which he shares about when he went to heaven. We had a great church service afterwards which he very much enjoyed.

He went back to Denmark a saved and changed man. He told me he would continue to attend the Lutheran church he was going to. My heart was at peace and assured that he was saved.

We kept in touch a few times over the years until I went into full time ministry. At the back of my mind I was at peace about him although my shift into ministry meant somehow I was not able to keep as much in touch with him as I did.

Early in January 2012, I received an email in my inbox which elicited anguish and sorrow in my heart. The email was from his work colleague saying Eigil had died of cancer very suddenly. As I was seized with grief in my heart (I had not known he had cancer) I felt the Lord whisper to me to remember the day he sat with me at a restaurant and accepted Him in his heart. Because of that he was with Him in heaven.

Although the Lord tried to assure me, I was still very sad that I had not kept in touch with him up till the end. A month later, my grief was taken away when his sister called me and told me that Eigil had called her years ago to tell her of his experience with Jesus in that restaurant. Not only that, but right till the very end she assured me he kept his faith with Jesus. I started to cry tears

of joy and I asked her if she would like to experience what her brother had till the end. She said yes and I led her to the Lord on the phone. What peace she had in her heart.

This surely must be a valuable lesson to Christians to take full advantage of the urgency of our times. Jesus admonishes us to take full advantage of these end times and the time of darkness we are in by preaching the gospel to all nations. Wherever we are in the market place or in the nations we can all do this.

What lesson can we as believers learn from the story of Eigil?

1. We are able to minister Jesus in whatever sphere of influence we are placed in. For those working in a business environment that are filled with the Spirit of God and a zeal to minister the love of Jesus to the lost, while care can be taken to focus on work during office hours, there is nothing wrong with building friendships with work colleagues and sharing Jesus with them during lunch or social hours.

2. We must take full advantage of the Spirit's prompting within us especially when we have an urgent leading to witness to someone. We must cast fear aside in such circumstances. I could easily have been afraid of an adverse reaction to ministering Jesus to a company customer who I was involved with professionally, as he might possibly have taken offence and reported me at work. God who sees all things saw into the future that his end was near and he knew that was an opportunity that had to be taken advantage of and not allowed to slip away. When faced with such an occasion of the Spirit's prompting we must be bold as our decision could have a life or death effect on the person we are being led to minister to.

3. When we are faced with a similar circumstance, there are certain things we can do to ensure successful witnessing

to the individual we are being led to speak to. We should endeavour to pray before-hand before witnessing to the person if we have the opportunity do so. In this situation we prayed specifically that God would remove the veil from Eigil's eyes and heart, and that he would receive the gospel without rejecting it due to the reasoning in his mind. God answered that prayer exactly as I prayed.

4. We can always believe God for a common ground to witness to the person we are in business with or have any type of relationship with. I found my common ground by talking about what makes him happy and that allowed me to subsequently share what brought happiness into my life and lead him to the Lord. Praying for him beforehand with my church team had ensured that God had opened his heart beforehand and removed his veil of delusion and so when I spoke to him he was ready to receive.

5. When we see signs that a person is ready to receive Jesus as Lord and Saviour, we must take advantage of this by asking the person if he is ready to receive the Lord. If the person answers yes, we can lead them in the salvation prayer where they ask God to forgive their sins and receive Jesus within their heart. When a person shows signs of being open to receive the gospel we can go ahead, confirm that decision with the person and lead them to the Lord as that opportunity has been created for that purpose.

Today, Eigil is in heaven with Jesus and through this story being told about him, I hope believers reading this can understand and flow with the urgency of the times we are in and be the eyes and ears of Jesus. It was also my intention to use this story and this chapter to share practical tips on how we can effectively witness

for the Lord regardless of where we serve. We must always take advantage of every opportunity because of the urgency of the times we are in.

If Satan is cognizant of the times we are in and seeks to make the world darker and uglier with sin, then we can determine to be a step ahead of him by letting our light shine as we witness and bring an increase of the light of God everywhere we go.

I believe we live in amazing and pivotal times where anyone willing to run with the heart of Jesus will receive specially prepared mantles to run their race and bring in the harvest. Heaven is waiting to pour out His Spirit and He will not disappoint. God is accelerating destinies for divine purpose.

One of the ways I have seen the Lord accelerate purpose and destinies into people's lives is by impartation. It could either happen by a person's hunger igniting an impartation to be ignited into their lives or by the laying on of hands.

> *"For this reason I remind you to fan into flame the gift of God, which is in you through the laying on of my hands".*
>
> 2 Timothy 1: 6

Last year, I was ministering at a church in the Netherlands called the Source of Living Waters Church. In one of the sessions where I made an altar call, an eleven year old boy came forward to give his life to Jesus. We all rejoiced when he did so. During the question and answers time, I asked if anyone had any question to ask and Joel put up his hand. I waited expectantly and this was the question he asked.

"If Jesus came into my heart, how come I don't feel Him in my heart; how do I know He really is there"?

We all laughed when he asked that question and I wondered at the unashamed honesty of the very young. I answered his question by explaining that there are things we do not see that exist. For example, we speak, think and eat because we have a soul even though we do not see it. So God exists even though we do not see Him. The proof of what He has created is surely proof that He exists. I also explained to Joel that God keeps His words and if He says He will come into our heart when we ask Him then that is what He does.

I could almost feel the wheels turning in his head even as I explained this to him but he still looked very uncertain and not quite believing what I said. He desperately wanted to feel the presence of God at his young age. Trusting that God would answer his question and give him rest, I continued with the service.

At the time of impartation, I asked for those who wanted an impartation of the fire of the Lord and boldness for the harvest to come forward. Several came forward and lined up in front as I started to pray. I looked to my left in front and I saw Joel beginning to shake and twitch under the presence of God even with no one laying hands on him! He soon fell on the floor under God's power where he shook as if electricity currents were running through his body. It soon became apparent that he had a major encounter with God that day because of what happened afterwards. His grandmother later emailed me to say that on the way home with Joel in the car, he started to sing a new song about Jesus being in his heart and said 'Grandma, I can't wait to go to school and tell everyone about Jesus'

That afternoon, Joel had an encounter with God and a young evangelist was born. The impartation he received on the day he got saved allowed him to be accelerated into his call or destiny

as a soul winner for Jesus. In various meetings I ministered at, I heard those who testified of having encounters with God through the laying on of hands. Some had been very timid before but became on fire soul winners for Jesus. God is allowing this to happen more and more because of the urgency of the times we are in.

I also want to share what I believe to be the key ingredient that helps us to be effective witnesses for Jesus.

I believe a key factor in being an effective witness for Jesus is understanding and knowing the heart of God; His heart does not change as God is the same today, yesterday and forever. If we can understand God's heart, then we will understand that His heart literally pumps and beats with love for souls. If we know God then we seek to be involved in what He loves the most.

> *"This is what the Lord says: "Let not the wise boast of their wisdom or the strong boast of their strength or the rich boast of their riches, but let the one who boasts boast about this: that they have the understanding to know me, that I am the Lord, who exercises kindness, justice and righteousness on earth, for in these I delight, declares the Lord".* Jeremiah 9:23-24

> *"For God so loved the world that he gave his one and only Son, that whoever believes in him shall not perish but have eternal life.".* John 3:16

> *"Do I take any pleasure in the death of the wicked? declares the sovereign LORD. Rather, am I not pleased when they turn from their ways and live?"* Ezekiel 18: 23

Both the Old and New Testament are in agreement about the nature of God in that He delights in saving mankind and He takes no pleasure in the damnation of man.

I had this fact brought home to me vividly as I preached in a chapel of a Ugandan women's prison in 2008. I had preached a message of love, restoration and hope and at the end I made an altar call to the women who wanted to give their lives to Jesus. A few women initially came forward. I felt in my Spirit there were many more who needed Jesus as Saviour but were afraid to come out. So I kept declaring that no matter what they had done that God would forgive them if they would turn to Him that day in repentance.

As I made the altar call again, more women came forward and gave their lives to Jesus. I noticed that one of these women kept sobbing uncontrollably as she accepted Christ in her heart. When I asked my interpreter at the end, she said the woman was sobbing because she had murdered a young person and yet God forgave her. She had initially not wanted to come out to give her heart to Jesus as she had found it very difficult to believe that God could forgive her.

The truth is the blood of Jesus was shed for everyone and for every sin and the nature of God remains the same that He delights in salvation and not the death of a wicked man. We can be confident that God is willing to save everyone who turns to him. This should make us confident to share the gospel with everyone.

Now that we know God's heart, it is necessary to have His heart within us. Sometimes it is easier to reach out or want to preach the gospel to a certain people because we understand them more or have an affinity with them. For some other groups of people, it seems more difficult to minister to them as we do not understand them or have a heart for them. Earlier on in this book, I shared how the Lord gave me a heart to love Muslims

and how an outpouring of God's power from that place of love brought a wonderful harvest of souls amongst them.

In 2008, I signed up to be part of the mission trip with Extreme Prophetic Ministries in Pattaya, Thailand. It was a mission trip to minister to the prostitutes and those at the heart of the sex industry. It was also an outreach school that was aimed to train us on how to reach out to those in the sex industry. Prior to this trip, I already loved everyone and had no problem ministering to those God asked me to minister to. Yet I found that when I had encountered prostitutes in the past I had not understood them at all and I would not say I even had a heart for them. I loved them as I loved others but my attitude was one that often wondered why they would be so foolish to sell their bodies for money, so I had little sympathy for them.

The outreach at Pattaya thankfully was preceded by a training school which served to expose my heart attitude in contrast with God's heart for His creation which had gone into prostitution. We also got to hear the background of how a lot of the girls had gone into prostitution and that broke my heart more than anything. I understood that a lot of these girls were victims in so many ways.

The Lord created them and they were perfect in how He made them, but the course of their destiny had been tampered with by the evil one who had caused them to be led astray with the belief system that they had no intrinsic value in themselves, except from the money value they could fetch with selling their bodies.

Many of them were sold as children into prostitution. Some parents actively encouraged their daughters from the time they were young that prostitution was a lucrative and desirable way of making money. Even sadder were those that were called 'lady

boys'. They had been born as males but had either undergone a sex change to become girls and practice prostitution or while still having male bodies, were happy to dress as girls and practice prostitution.

We also learned that some of these lady boys had been encouraged by their parents while they were still young to go into this path since being a girl was a more profitable way of making money as a prostitute. We could hardly contain ourselves as we wept profusely at the sadness of the stories we heard. My heart began to beat with new found compassion, love and understanding for these people.

By receiving the heart of Jesus for them, it became my natural instinct to show the love of Jesus to these girls, who night after night sold their bodies for money hoping that one night the next man who came would be their knight in shining armour and would take them away from all that. Jesus is their true knight who has already paid a price to woo them to be His bride. He loves them as they are and they do not have to pay anything to receive the salvation, deliverance and restoration He so freely has for them. By receiving this truth within their hearts, a new path of freedom from sin and shame was set in motion.

The school developed a strategy where night after night we would go to the bars and clubs where they worked and onto the streets and befriend the girls. Jesus truly is a friend of sinners so we took time to listen to them, build friendship and relationship with them and in doing so also revealed the heart of Jesus to them. They realised we were not out to judge or condemn them but that we had come as friends with a heart of Jesus for them.

The friendship we built with them helped them to put their walls aside and to listen with interest when we spoke about

Jesus and several of them did give their lives to Jesus and many came off the streets to become part of the Tamar Center, an institution that exists in Pattaya that helps to rehabilitate and take care of those who had practiced prostitution. In this center, they learned English and other skills that could give them gainful employment.

Often when I share on Prophetic Evangelism in training Schools, I use this example which reveals God's heart in a very powerful way.

One of the strategies of bringing the bar girls to the Lord was to hold a banquet in one of the hotels and prepare food in a wonderful celebratory environment. We would treat them like princesses that night because that is how they are made to be in Christ before the enemy tampered with their destiny and that is how we saw them.

For those of us who stayed behind in the banquet halls, we were busy praying for the night event and for the girls who were going to come in. As we prayed, we were encouraged to ask and believe God for a picture or a word for those we were going to meet and minister to. The banquet hall itself was laid out in such a way that each person attending the outreach school was a table host. As the table host we would be responsible for taking care of those who sat at our table. Those were the ones for whom we were encouraged to believe for a word from the Lord.

As I closed my eyes and began to pray with others believing for a word or picture from God, I saw a picture begin to form of a lady who would walk into the meeting with an inordinate amount of what looked like diamanté stones on her face. Her eyelashes, nose, ears and parts of her face had an extreme amount of glittering stuff on it. I heard the Lord tell me that when I met

her I should let her know that she was more precious to Him than all the diamantes she had on her body. That was a very profound statement because for someone who had no value in herself except for the monetary value she could get from selling her body, those diamantes as her possession must have meant a lot to her. I guess they made her feel beautiful too. For her to hear that she was more precious to the Lord regardless of the lifestyle she had lived would be a profound statement to her indeed.

I closed my eyes and continued to pray and the Lord told me I was going to meet another lady who was extremely worried about her future but that I should tell her that if she would commit her future into His hands and trust Him that He would take care of it. She need not worry any longer. It was a very simple word but I felt sure that for the Lord to have highlighted the word that it would mean a lot to her when she hears the word.

Soon we finished praying and many girls started to come in. They came in excitedly like kids hardly believing the extent to which we had prepared to lavish them with love in such beautiful surroundings. We all stood by our different tables waiting for those who the Lord was going to lead us to.

I looked and I saw a lady come in who had an extraordinary amount of diamanté stones on part of her face just like I saw in the vision and she came straight to my table! Everyone the Lord had given me a word for ended up sitting at my table. God's plans are always perfect and if we trust in Him He will bring to pass everything He has shown us.

As the ladies sat on the table I was hosting, I did not immediately give them the prophetic words. I knew it was important to build friendship with them first. We talked and chatted about various things while they ate and danced to the music being played. At

the time we were asked to minister to the ladies, I approached the ones I had the words for and told them what the Lord had laid on my heart to give them. How their hearts melted! I remember a lady weeping profusely as she was confronted with the love of God. Several ladies around my table and others gave their hearts to Jesus that night.

I believe the encounter with these ladies happened because the Lord gave us His heart for them. If anyone reading this book has struggled with ministering to a certain type of people, be encouraged that the Lord has shed His perfect love abroad in your hearts with which you are able to love others. You can also ask the Lord to give you a heart of love, understanding and compassion to be able to love those He has called you to love into the kingdom. In order to enter into the rest and ease for this work of the end time harvest, we need to possess the same heart that Jesus has for everyone regardless of their sin, nature, religion or nationalities. We must not let anything stand in the way of releasing His love to those who Jesus loves so much. We must be a friend to all just as much as Jesus was.

Sensitivity is another key factor to how we witness and can often determine the outcome of a person's choice for salvation. The Holy Spirit is the one who convicts souls to be saved but with our sensitivity to the Holy Spirit, we can be at the right place and the right time when ministering to people.

When we are sensitive to the Holy Spirit, we can also be aware of when the timing is appropriate to build or develop a relationship before sharing the word. Instigating a friendship does not necessarily have to take weeks, it could be an hour or thirty minutes but the important thing is to know when some have some walls that needs to be dealt with by love and patience

before the word we speak can minister to them.

I remembered a Chinese lady I met at a bus stop several years ago on my way to work. I smiled at her and I was really friendly asking how she was. I made a point to chat with her each time I met her on the way to work. We exchanged phone numbers and soon arranged to meet for dinner. We met at a nice restaurant for a meal after which I invited her to my place which was nearby.

We chatted and she told me the reason why she became so open to me was because I smiled at her all the time I met her at the bus stop even when others seemed so stressed out and never smiled. She was interested in knowing me more and that night was a divine moment because this precious lady gave her heart to the Lord. She told me she had been approached many times about Jesus and had even been given a Bible, but that was the first time she had ever given her heart to Him.

I was sensitive to the flow of the Spirit as to how the Lord wanted to bring about this lady's salvation and it was through building a friendship which started with a smile at a bus stop.

I had already mentioned that being sensitive to the Holy Spirit meant I could sometimes sense when there was not much time in building a friendship with the unsaved person I met before I shared the gospel with them, so there is no hard and fast rule. We become seasoned in our sensitivity to the Holy Spirit the more we yield to him in obedience. Many times I have just simply been led to a person, smiled and quickly shared the love of Jesus and His gospel with them. Because of the authority Jesus has given me to walk in, there have been many salvations in these short instances also, as the Holy Spirit ministered to hearts with His convicting power and presence.

The urgency of the times we live in means that we must become seasoned in our sensitivity to the Holy Spirit with those who are ready to be reaped or harvested into the kingdom of God. The Lord is releasing such grace that within five minutes I have seen the Lord bring a person to salvation.

There was a really funny story that happened in early 2012. I was on my way to attend a pastors and leaders meeting at Oasis Church in London when I became really hungry on the way. I walked into a shop and asked for a pack of unsalted peanuts. I had started a diet which meant I was eating the healthiest foods. The shopkeeper replied and told me they only had salted peanuts. I wanted to walk away and not buy them when I felt an insistent urge in my Spirit to buy it anyway.

I walked out of the shop and saw a man walking on the street holding a bottle of drink in his hand who did not look hungry at all but I heard the leading of the Lord telling me to give my peanuts to him and that would be an avenue or a gateway for him to receive the Lord. I thought to myself 'That's just some random thought running through my mind, you just don't go around London offering peanuts to those who don't even look hungry'

I said hello and started talking to him anyway. We were on our way chatting when suddenly he said to me 'Well, you know if you give me your bag of peanuts, I'll give you my drink'

I looked at him stunned and told him that from the time I saw him that God had told me to offer him from my bag of peanuts. That proved an interesting turn of conversation, as he wondered whether God indeed told me that. Before walking away to where he was going, he took some of the peanuts I offered him and he received Jesus in his heart! I gave him the address of the church

that was holding the leaders meeting and he was keen to give it a go. Being sensitive to the leading of the Spirit can mean offering something as little as a bag of peanuts to open the gateway of a person's heart to receive Him. Quite often God will use what we have in our hands or gifts or talents that He's given us to open up the door of peoples' hearts to Him.

Another time the Lord used a pack of mince pies I had with me to open up the door of a heart to Him to be saved. One Sunday I had been worshipping at the Catch the Fire Church in London, just before Christmas when I noticed the pastor had a pack of mince pies with him. I detest mince pies myself as I do not like the taste! I took one from him any way and somehow during that night, I began to get a sense that the Lord was going to use what was in my hand to open doors of salvation that night.

As I walked home on the busy high street, I saw a man sitting on the street. He was hungry and asked if I could spare one of the mince pies I had with me. I responded by giving him one. He looked at me and said I was a walking Christian. By that act, he had identified me with Jesus who often fed the poor. I knew there was a deeper and more important hunger in him which must be satisfied. In simple words, I shared the gospel of Jesus with him and asked him if he would like to receive Jesus in his heart. He said yes and I led him to the Lord. As we continued to chat, one of his Italian lady friends came to sit with him and hearing what happened with her friend, she was encouraged and she also gave her heart to the Lord in prayer.

As a church, we must realise that every avenue to make the gospel known has been provided for us, be it through supernatural signs and wonders with the word of the gospel being spoken or through practical acts of kindness. We can make full use of

the ministry of reconciliation that has been committed into our hands.

Many years ago, I used to be part of a church choir but left because I did not feel that was God's calling for my life. I am quite happy to sing merrily as I take a walk on the streets much to the amusement and delight of passers-by. Some open doors I have had are a result of a passerby hearing me singing and wanting to know what I was singing about.

One day on my way to church I was singing a new song spontaneously about the river of God flowing from God's throne to heal every sick person. There were two guys sitting on a railing hearing me sing and one of them remarked that I had a lovely voice and he wanted to know what I was singing about. I told him I was singing about the river of God flowing to heal every sickness. He must have been bemused about that but he thought it was a lovely sentiment. I told him Jesus would come into his heart and forgive his sins if he was willing to invite Him in and right there on the street of London he invited Jesus into his heart.

If we are willing God will use every gift and talent He has given us to be a doorway for the spread of the gospel of Jesus. I feel He is asking someone reading this book: "What do you have in your hands?" like He did with the boy with the five loaves and two fishes.

Regardless of how small or insignificant you think the talent God has given you is, in the kingdom it is significant and the Lord will multiply and use your talent effectively to bring in the harvest if you will let Him.

Being light in this world and being an effective witness for Jesus can be so simple if we walk in the light of His leading and speak the words He gives us to the one who needs Him the most.

'The steps of the righteous are ordered by the Lord and he delights in his every way' Psalm 37:23 (Paraphrased).

One of the ways that can help increase our sensitivity to the Lord is to pray that the Lord direct our steps daily and open doors of opportunity for us to minister his love. We should also pray to recognise those doors when they are opened so we do not miss them.

About six or seven years ago, I entered a bus on my way to London; I was all dressed up in my business suit. I proceeded to look for a place to sit and noticed a man sitting in front wearing overalls that looked wet with paint. Instinctively, I was going to sit somewhere else as the wet paint might have rubbed off on my clothes but I sensed the Spirit prompting me to sit where he was and not to sit anywhere else. This is one of the times when I needed to act urgently within a short space of time.

I turned to him and said "hi" to him, telling him that Jesus loved him. He actually loved the idea that he was loved. I shared how Jesus loved him so much that He died and gave His life for him. I shared with him that Jesus was knocking on the door of his heart and wanted to know if he would let Him in. He said yes and prayed for Jesus to come into his heart. He smiled and thanked me for stopping to talk to him. It turned out he was getting off the next bus stop.

I was amazed that God knew where he was going to get off at and provided that opportune moment for him to hear about Jesus, a moment that might have been missed if I had not recognized or acknowledged the leading of the Lord. The truth is that when we pray this way for God to lead and guide our footsteps daily then we must be fully expectant that God will do exactly that.

One of the key factors to being an effective witness is also to recognise the activities of the angels around us. I believe there is such an increase of angelic activity for the work of the harvest especially in these end times. They have been sent to help us reap and bring in the harvest.

Hebrews 1:14 says:

> *"Are not all angels ministering Spirits sent to serve those who will inherit salvation?"*

Angels have been dispatched on the earth for the inheritors of salvation. I believe they are especially active around those who are at the point of being ready to receive Jesus. Usually, there have been a lot of intercessory prayers on their behalf. Then Lord releases these angels to nudge his saints to be answers to the unsaved who are at the point of receiving Him. Often angels even nudge the unsaved to come into contact or even approach His saints so that they can receive a word from them.

A few years ago, I had an experience where I had been to Speakers' Corner to minister. I had spoken to a few people and I had come to the end of my day so I was planning to leave. I was tired and wanted to go home when a man suddenly approached me. I had not spoken to him but he came to me and started to tell me the dilemma he was in. He said he was very depressed and had tried so many things to cure his depression but none of them worked.

He told me he was depressed because of a painful break up with his wife, which meant his children got taken away from him and he did not really see them. He told me lately he had been advised to try the church! I stared at him thinking if this was not a cry for help, then what else could it be. He was literally begging for help and I wondered how he knew I was a Christian since I had not

even spoken to him.

I discovered in the course of our conversation that he was from Lebanon. When he told me he had been advised to try the church, at that point I agreed and I told him I was a Christian and yes I agreed it was a good idea. I told him there was an evening service at the church I attended and asked him if he wanted to come. He said he would have come but he had already booked a ticket to go to the cinema that evening. Seeing that this was obviously a divine appointment, I took the liberty of advising him to cancel the cinema he had booked so he could come with me to the evening church service. He agreed and we walked across to the cinema together to cancel the booking.

When we got back to the Speakers' Corner, we stood and continued to talk. He told me he was so unhappy and had become depressed and that one of the signs of his depression was he would often have tears in his eyes whenever he spoke about his kids. I noticed that as I listened to him speak; his eyes were glinting with tears as he mentioned the dilemma of not having his kids with him anymore.

Filled with anger and anguish at the betrayal and hurt he had suffered from his wife, he suddenly looked at me and shouted 'I hate all women'. I knew he was suffering and told him that God did not cause his pain and God's plan was for a happy and beautiful marriage which the enemy wanted to destroy.

I told him my testimony of being saved and how the Lord saved me from depression in the process. I told him that all I said was a simple prayer of salvation and not only did that prayer save me from sin into eternal life but it also removed all depression from my heart and life.

The Lord must have imparted the gift of boldness to me because suddenly I told him that if he would give God a chance and say that same prayer of salvation asking God to forgive his sins and allowing Jesus to be his Lord and Saviour, then all depression would leave his heart just like it left me.

As soon as I said those words, I felt the enemy whispering to me that I had just told a tremendous lie; that the man would say the sinner's prayer but that nothing would change. He would still be as depressed as ever and worse still I would be known to be a liar. I knew these were the enemy's words and I went on to encourage the man to give Jesus a chance as he had tried everything else and what did he have to lose. He said the prayer of salvation and invited Jesus into his heart.

It was soon time for us to go to church and we went to the service together. He very much enjoyed the vibrant Kensington Temple Pentecostal service and afterwards when the service finished we stood outside the church to talk further. He went on for a while talking about his failed marriage as he was still angry. He talked about the disappointment of losing his kids too.

All the time I was looking at his eyes with interest and to my joy and delight, I noticed that his eyes were clear and that he had no tears in his eyes at all. I joyfully told him that he was healed of his depression because there had been no tears at all in his eyes all the time he had been talking about his kids.

God demonstrated the fulfilment of Isaiah 61 in the life of this precious man from Lebanon, who was not only saved but healed of his depression too.

As a further sign that he was healed, a few months after that day, I was at work when I heard my phone ring and he was on the other end of the phone thanking me for the way his life had turned out as he had been going to the church. He no longer suffered from

depression and felt entirely like a new man. I told him it was wholly Jesus who had saved and turned his life around and I was only the vessel that He had used to bring healing and salvation into his life.

There were several keys that were evident in the life of this man that we could all press into our daily walk with Jesus to bring in the harvest.

1. One was the influence of the angelic around this man who had nudged him (although he was unaware) to take a step towards my direction even as I was at the point of leaving the square.
2. Another key was the fact that I recognized meeting him as a divine appointment and I acknowledged it by allowing God to meet his needs at the time.
3. Another factor here was the gift of faith that was in operation that made me declare to him so boldly that he would instantly be healed of depression if he was to give his life to Jesus. Normally, what might have happened in other circumstances was that I could have led a person to the Lord who was suffering from depression and afterwards pray for him to be healed but in this instance, I had declared boldly to him that he would be totally healed of the chronic depression that he was suffering from immediately at the point of salvation. That was the gift of faith in operation and I even told him that as a sign that he was healed he would never cry or have tears in his eyes when he spoke of his kids again all of which he had told me had been impossible before.

Let us not be afraid to take a step of faith or operate in the gift of faith when the Lord is using us to minister to the unsaved because He will honour our faith if we trust in Him.

Determining to walk in faith and love are key ingredients that help us to respond effectively to God's need as we minister to the unsaved in the urgent times we are in.

Determination to not only walk in the light but to be ready to release the light of God within us to those we meet is very much a key to being an effective witness for Jesus. It is also true that opportunities to demonstrate faith and love and to be salt and light can happen at any moment, even in circumstances we do not expect.

Another time recently I felt that another man had been nudged by an angel to approach me and it happened as I was walking from the hospital. It was a very chilly night in London and I did not have my gloves on. It was one of those cold nights that the chilling temperature actually hurt my skin as I walked.

As I walked, a man walked alongside me and wondered aloud that I did not have a pair of gloves on such a cold night. He told me it was really cheap to get a pair of gloves that would protect me from being sick on such a cold night. Of course I knew he was right in a practical way but wanting to make conversation in a way that would make him think about God, I told him that I believed that God would protect me in that terrible cold and prevent me from being ill.

Realising I was a Christian, he told me his grandma had often admonished him to receive Jesus in his heart which he had not done. As we talked, his bus suddenly passed by and he seemed so upset. He said to me' Oh no, I have missed my bus' I looked at him and told him that while it was sad that he missed his bus, it would not be as bad as if he missed the opportunity to receive Jesus. I asked him what good it would be if he gained the whole world but lost his own soul.

He looked at me sadly and he said he thought he would lose his soul anyway or had lost it already. I told him he surely had an opportunity that night from an ever-loving God, that he had not lost his soul, and how wonderful it would be if he would make a way for Jesus in his heart.

He asked me how he could do that and I told him he only needed to repent of his sins from the heart and ask forgiveness from God and ask Jesus in his heart. He prayed on the street to receive Jesus as Lord and Saviour. I still had time so I connected him to a church where he could fellowship and grow.

As we finished, his bus came. He entered it looking like a different person. He looked so happy and declared that Jesus was in his heart. How easy all this seems but this is what happens when in our everyday life we surrender totally to the workings of Jesus to reach out to those who need Him the most. Our lives become a daily adventure of miracles, signs and wonders as we operate in holy boldness for our King.

> *"The people walking in darkness have seen a great light; on those living in the land of deep darkness a light has dawned."*
> Isaiah 9:2

This prophecy was fulfilled at the appearing of Jesus when He came into the world as the light and the darkness in the lives of people was dispersed because of Him, as He healed and delivered many and through His ultimate sacrifice, salvation came into the world.

Today, we are the extensions of the arm of Jesus on this earth and He longs to demonstrate His light so that people sitting in great darkness and in absolute misery can see the light of Jesus through us.

I had another opportunity to shine the light of Jesus on a man that was sitting in darkness in the most ordinary of circumstances this year. I was taking a walk along in neighbourhood. I had taken to doing power walking regularly in my neighbourhood to keep fit and this aerobic exercise in the form of rigorous walking is a favoured form of exercise for the British.

I had finished my walk and was on my way home when I noticed what seemed to be a commotion in front of me. A number of people seemed to be gathered around a man that was on the floor. I walked closer to this man and noticed that he was bleeding profusely from his head. It turned out that as he had been walking, he had fallen and hit his head on the floor. He had a gash on his head and a lady called an ambulance. By any means this man was sitting in the darkness, in the valley of the shadow of death and I was filled with compassion as I looked at him.

I approached him and thankfully he was lucid. I asked him if he needed prayers and he nodded and welled up with tears. The ambulance arrived before I could pray for him and as the paramedics picked him up I asked the man if I could come with him into the ambulance and he said yes. I believe that when we move in obedience to the leading of the Lord to be light to the suffering, we will also receive favour to minister to them.

The Lord gave me favour with the man even though I was unknown to him and not his family. I watched and listened to the paramedics as they asked about his family but he could not seem to give them any those details. He seemed so alone.

When there was a moment of quietness as the paramedics took their notes, I spoke to the man and asked if it was okay to pray for him and again he said yes. I explained to him as gently and patiently as possible repeating the fact that Jesus loved him,

cared about him and would come into his heart and save him if he could ask for forgiveness and receive him as his Lord and personal Saviour.

There was a poignant openness in his heart and he agreed to say a pray for Jesus to forgive him and come into his heart. It was a joyful moment and my heart was glad for him.

At that time, I could have walked off the ambulance which had not started moving yet and walked home but I had a feeling the work God wanted me to do was not completely done yet. The paramedics asked me if I was accompanying him into the hospital and again he gave an acknowledgement to them that he was okay with that. They told me they would not be able to bring me back home if I decided to go with them in the ambulance.

Although I had only a pound with me which was not enough to take a bus fare home, somehow I trusted God to take care of that part of my journey and affirmed to them that I would be accompanying him into the hospital.

The man was so grateful that he reached out to hug me and in the process some of the blood on him got on my clothes and skin but I was past caring, I just seemed to be more and more filled with Jesus during that adventure that night. I believe he saw Jesus in me that night too and all he wanted to do was reach out to the One who had been so kind to him through me.

We arrived at the accident and emergency department of the hospital. As he was led into the waiting room to sit, I saw people who were there who had been brought in a lot of agony. Others were being brought in with their face streaming with blood and in obvious pain.

I started to have even more of a sense of being on a divine assignment that night as I saw more and more people being

attended to who were in pain and my compassion levels kept on increasing.

Generally in accident wards of hospitals in England, only friends or relatives are allowed into rooms or wards of those who are being attended to and the patient's privacy is usually guarded.

I believed that night the Lord covered me and hid me in His secret place underneath the shadow of His wings because of the assignment He had for me that night. I began to feel a pull of the Spirit to minister and help those who were in such pain. I began to enter the rooms of those who were waiting for surgery or waiting to be seen and started to talk to them to find out what happened to them and just generally love on them to try to ease their pain.

The amazing thing was they all spoke to me individually as if they had known me for a long time when in reality I was neither their friend nor family! They opened up and each told me how they got to be in the state they were in. When I tried to leave one of the rooms, one of the men with the bloodied face stopped me and begged me not to leave the room but to stay and talk to him some more. His surgeon was about to come in to perform the surgery on his cut head and I knew I had to act quickly as I might never see him again. Within the few moments I had, I told him the most important message of the gospel; that he was loved by a loving Saviour called Jesus Who died for him on the cross.

I told him Jesus wanted to save him from pain and sin and if he would allow Jesus and welcome Him in his heart in repentance and sincerity, Jesus would honour his prayers and come into his heart and save him. He was ever so willing and invited Jesus as Lord and Saviour into his heart just before the surgeon came in and I had to leave his room!

We should always make use of such opportunities the Lord gives us to the uttermost and not waste it as He wants to give every single person on this earth a chance to know Him or hear of Him and we are the vessels He uses to do so.

I spoke with a few other suffering patients till it got quite late in the hospital. Suddenly, the hospital nurses looked at me and commented 'Surely, you cannot be related to all these people whose rooms you are entering'.

Their hospital protocol had been broken and they were not even aware of it. The Lord had supernaturally hidden from them what was happening. The fact that I was not related to those whose rooms I was entering should have been apparent from the beginning but the Lord hid me from their usual alert gaze because He wanted to use me that night on an assignment to touch lives of those who might otherwise not have heard the gospel again. I like to think of that episode in the hospital as a secret agent assignment for the Lord!

Not only were my activities hidden from the hospital workers, He also gave me favour with the patients that I spoke to. Without that favour, His ministry through me would not have been received with such openness from the patients. By the time the nurses noticed what was happening, it was too late but I felt I had completed the assignment that night.

It was time for me to go home but I still had only a pound with me which was not enough to take me home. One of the ladies I was talking to, who had accompanied one of the patients, stretched forth her hands and gave me two pounds. It was the exact amount of money that I needed to take me home in addition to what I already had.

The Lord had taken care of every part of that journey that night from beginning to the end, as He will do for every single one who decides to walk in obedience to do His will. If He has called you, He will make provision for you to take care of your every need.

If you are reading this book and you know you have been called to minister in very difficult or possibly dangerous places, lay your hands on your chest as you receive this prayer

'Father, I pray that your abiding secret place in Psalm 91 will make provision for hiddeness for your people, that as they go about the assignment you have laid on their heart to do, they will be protected from all evil.

I pray that they will be hidden from all evil eyes and kept from every act of distraction that could stop or hinder them in the assignment you have called them into.

Father, grant them favour in every way, that those they have been called to minister to, even those in high governmental places, can receive the ministry of Jesus with gladness and eagerness in their hearts. I pray this in the name of your precious son Jesus Christ of Nazareth. Amen!

The last key I wanted to share is that of prayer and intercession. This has been a running theme throughout this book so I will not say much here but it's worth summarizing this very important key here. Every move of God has always been preceded by prayer and to be effective witnesses for Jesus, we must constantly live and operate in the realm of prayer.

Prayer is what opens the heart of the unsaved. Prayer is what releases the soul of the unsaved from demonic strongholds so they can be free to make decisions to receive Jesus. Angels are sent on assignment in answers to our prayers to minister on behalf of those who are to be heirs of salvation. Prayers move

the hands of God to release revival and prophetic decrees help to establish God's will on earth and to establish His kingdom. Through our decrees, every valley of dry bones can become a living army of saved people for Jesus Christ.

Be encouraged with everything that has been made available to you today which includes the blood of Jesus, the power and convicting power of the Holy Spirit, the presence of the Lord and everything heaven has laid down for our disposal. Make every effort not to be found wanting in the calling on your life for this end time harvest. Let us count the cost as our Lord and Saviour did when He laid down his life for us, and make every opportunity count to be salt and light to this world that so desperately needs Jesus.

It is my hope and prayer that by reading this book, boldness and encouragement have been imparted to your heart and the keys I have shared in this book will release God's kingdom on earth to help lead the souls of men from eternal torment to becoming a habitation of the King of Kings and Lord of Lords.

As you encounter and minister the gospel to those you meet, it is my prayer that their hearts will be convicted by the Holy Spirit to receive Jesus as Saviour and Lord in repentance and faith. The prayer below is a helpful guideline you can encourage them to pray below. May you all reap the reward of following the Lamb of God,

God, I acknowledge my sins. Please forgive my sins.
I believe that Jesus died for me and rose from the dead, and I'm thankful for what He has done for me.
Jesus, please come into my heart and life and be my Lord and Saviour. Give me the grace and power to follow you all my days.
Thank you, Jesus

ABOUT THE AUTHOR

Ella Onakoya is the founder of Harvest of the Nations, a ministry based in London, England. She travels extensively as a full-time itinerant Evangelist and Prophetic Revivalist to many nations across the world. Ella preaches a message of revival and awakening that God is releasing to the nations through speaking at conferences, holding equipping schools and preaching at evangelistic crusades. Many have experienced salvations, physical healings and personal breakthroughs at her meetings.

At equipping schools held in many churches and ministries, Ella teaches on Spirit-led evangelism with a focus on hearing the heart of God and communicating it to the unsaved. She passionately believes the church is an army of everyday believers who have been called to transform communities and nations by living a supernaturally natural life every day. To help believers live such a life, Ella trains and equips them to move in supernatural gifts and signs and wonders as well as in prayer and spiritual warfare.

You can contact Ella Onakoya at the email below or if you wish to invite her to speak at your church.

email: info@harvestofthenations.com
website: www.harvestofthenations.com

Spirit Led Evangelism is also available on www.amazon.com, www.amazon.co.uk and in some bookstores near you.

Made in the USA
Columbia, SC
02 June 2020

10079644R00112